Christmas is Coming

The origins of our Christmas traditions and some of
the stories and legends which surround them

by

Monica Evans

Christmas is coming, the geese are getting fat,
Please to put a penny in the old man's hat.
If you haven't got a penny, a ha'penny will do,
If you haven't got a ha'penny, then God bless you!

A traditional rhyme

Pen Press

© Monica Evans 2009

All rights reserved

No part of this publication may be reproduced, stored in a retrieval system, or transmitted in any form or by any means, without the prior permission in writing of the publisher, nor be otherwise circulated in any form of binding or cover other than that in which it is published and without a similar condition including this condition being imposed on the subsequent purchaser.

First published in Great Britain by Pen Press

All paper used in the printing of this book has been made from wood grown in managed, sustainable forests.

ISBN13: 978-1-906710-36-1

Printed and bound in the UK
Pen Press is an imprint of Indepenpress Publishing Limited
25 Eastern Place
Brighton
BN2 1GJ

A catalogue record of this book is available from
the British Library

Cover design by the author Monica Evans

CHRISTMAS IS COMING

Monica Evans, was born in Suffolk, she studied at the Coventry School of Art and the Birmingham School of Speech and Drama and later became a student at the Birmingham Repertory Theatre.

She has worked in the theatre both as an actress and a designer, specialising in costume design and has also worked in America as a Drama Counsellor.

Whilst her children were young she taught art, drama and English in several Midland schools.

For many years now she has worked as a freelance lecturer giving entertaining and informative talks to diverse groups and societies including The National Trust and English Heritage. Her subject matter includes talks about herbs, wild plants, our traditional British festivals and, in particular, Christmas with it's associated plants, greenery, customs and festivities on which she is an authority.

She has appeared on television and radio speaking about the origins of our now familiar Christmas.

At present she lives with her husband in rural Warwickshire and in her spare time continues to paint and write poetry.

Medieval mummers

Dedication

For my husband John, whose enthusiasm for the Christmas season remains undiminished by the passing years and without whose help this book would never have been completed.

"At Ewle, we wanton gambole, dance to caviole and to sing, to have gud spice stewe and roste and plum pies for a king"

William Warner (1550)

Contents

List of Illustrations	viii
Introduction	ix
Advent	1
Christmas	14
Green Grow'th The Holly	22
Mistletoe	28
Father Christmas or Santa Claus ?	35
The Christmas Tree	46
Candles, Lamps and Lanterns	53
The Yule Log.	59
Christmas Cards	65
Robins	70
Carols and Mummers	75
Christmas Fare – puddings, mincepies and cakes	86
Turkeys, Geese and Christmas Meats	100
Crackers	110
Cribs	115
Gifts	120
Lords of Misrule, Masques and Pantomime	128
Games	138
Wassail	146
New Year's Eve - Hogmanay	150
The Abolition Of Christmas	163
Twelfth Night, Epiphany and Candlemas	174
Now Back To Work ! – Plough Monday and Distaff Day	183
Bibliography	189
Acknowledgements	191

List of Illustrations

Medieval Mummers	Monica Evans
Nativity	.. ..
"Make we merry ..."	.. ..
A Green Father Christmas (1880's)	
Nineteenth century print of Old Father Christmas	
Queen Victoria's Christmas Tree	The Illustrated London News 1848
The first known Christmas card	John Horsley (1843)?
World War 1 embroidered card (1914-18)	
"Nowell sing we ......"	Monica Evans
Ministry of Food wartime Christmas recipe leaflets (1942 - 45)	
Mrs Cratchit's Christmas Pudding An illustration for "A Christmas Carol"	R. Seymour
Mr Fezziwig's Ball An original print for Charles Dicken's "A Christmas Carol"	John Leech
Somerset Wassail Bowl	John Evans
A Vindication of Christmas, 17th century pamphlet	
The Tryal of Father Christmas, 1735 broadsheet.	
Decorated plough and Christmas faggot	John Evans

The cover and all other illustrations are by the author.

Introduction

Since early childhood I have been interested in my country's history and intrigued by seasonal traditions and folklore. I was a curious child and wanted to know WHY!

"Why do we put up holly at Christmas?", "Why do we kiss under mistlctoe?", "Why is a Principal Boy a girl?", "What is a Jack-o-the-Green" and "Why do we have Easter eggs?"

The adults I questioned rarely gave me any satisfactory answers and so gradually through the years I researched and read more and more about our British traditions. I discovered that I was not the only one interested in such subjects and so began giving talks and lectures on our folklore and traditions to like-minded people. Afterwards, many of my audience would often ask, "Have you written a book which we could purchase?"

Well now I have and whilst this book limits itself to the customs and traditions which surround the Christmas season, I hope it may provide some answers and enjoyment to those of you who, like me, value this particular time of the year without all the distractions of modern life.

Our past and present traditions – for traditions are constantly evolving - are a precious part of our heritage for they have contributed to our national character and help us to understand and appreciate our long dead ancestors' hopes, fears and superstitions which were connected to their everyday lives.

Long may our ancient customs continue to thrive and be handed down to future generations.

Monica Evans
2009

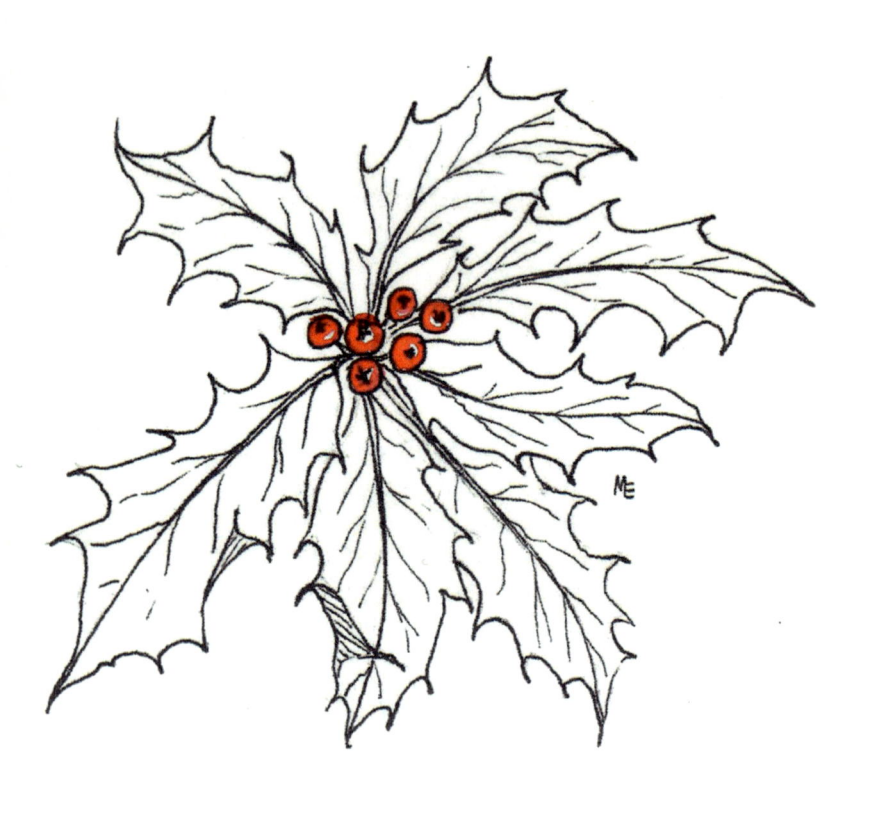

"The holly bears a berry as red as any blood..."

1

ADVENT

"Nowell... it is the tyme which is properlye called Advente."

13th Century monk of England.

Four weeks to go! Hurry now it's time to clean and bake,
Light the candles, mark off the days,
Stir the pudding, make the cake.
Cards need posting, presents bought without delay.
Advent, the time of preparation for joyous Christmas Day.

Anon

Advent is often more exciting and atmospheric than the actual period of our Christmas festivities. It is the "getting ready time" a busy and often frenetic four weeks which can be exhausting especially for shopkeepers, catering staffs and mothers. There are presents to buy and pack, cards to be written, food to be brought and prepared, houses made spic and span; carols ring out, Christmas markets abound, there are concerts and pantomimes to attend and very excited small children to contend with. Much of this has little to do with the spiritual preparation for the arrival of the Christ Child, which is the true meaning of Advent. We are all so busy that we lose sight of the original purpose of this very special time.

The word ADVENT is derived from the latin word AVENTUS meaning arrival. The season of Advent begins on the Sunday nearest to the thirtieth of November, which happens to be Saint Andrew's Day, and continues until December 24th, Christmas Eve, thus encompassing the four Sundays which precede Christmas. The first day of Advent (Advent Sunday) marks the beginning of each new ecclesiastical year, although in the Eastern Church the season of Advent is much longer than ours and begins in the middle of November. In the past Advent, like Lent, was celebrated by fasting, i.e. no meat was eaten, prior to the great feast of Christmas, except on Sundays which were exempt, but gradually this custom died out. Bishop Perpetuus of Tours (461-490) writes of a fast that began before Christmas on Saint Martin's Day (November 11th) and the solemnization of marriage was forbidden during this season by the Roman Catholic Church.

In recent years the wonderful Advent Carol Services have been revived in many of our larger churches and cathedrals. They take place on the first Sunday in Advent (Advent Sunday), which usually falls at the end of November.

The service itself is a journey from darkness to light symbolising the expected coming of light to the world with the Christ Child at Christmas. The church building is plunged into darkness and stillness as the service commences and then flickering candles are seen at the chancel end of the church and the distant voices of the choir are heard singing an Advent hymn. Gradually they process through the church from the east end, stopping at various points when the congregation's candles are lit by the clergy as they pass by. Slowly light spreads right through the building until it is a mass of glowing candlelight piercing the darkness of the winter night. Eventually the choir and clergy complete their journey around the church returning to the High Altar. It is a magical occasion with the choir singing their ancient carols, the soft candlelight, plus the feeling of joy and expectation for the coming Christmastide. Once experienced such a service is never forgotten.

Several saint's days are celebrated during the season of Advent and most of them have interesting stories and traditions connected with their particular feast days.

Dec 4th SAINT BARBARA

Saint Barbara's day falls on December 4th. Legend tells us that she was shut up in a tower by her father in order to keep her safe from unwanted suitors. However, she, unknown to him, had become a Christian. When her father discovered this he angrily denounced her to the authorities who tortured her, but she refused to renounce her faith. Barbara's father was then ordered to kill her himself and this he did; however, he was immediately struck by lightning and instantly killed. Because of this story Saint Barbara became the patroness of those threatened by storms lightning and explosions. Gunners and miners later adopted her as their patron saint and to this day she remains the patroness of artillery companies.

On her feast day French children used to sprinkle wheat seeds into shallow dishes containing a piece of damp flannel or soil. The dishes were kept warm and watered so that the wheat germinated and sprouted. On Christmas Eve great feasts were held and these dishes of sprouting wheat held pride of place on the tables as decorations. A similar custom takes place in Italy at Easter; the sprouting wheat represents new life and resurrection and the dishes are tied around with a narrow red ribbon which symbolises Christ's blood and sacrifice.

Small sprigs of early flowering trees such as cherry, plum or almond used to be cut on this day and taken inside, then placed in water so that the warmth of the house encouraged them to bloom in time for Christmas. Sprigs of flowering currant and forsythia can also be used to good effect in this way during the bleak days leading up to Christmas. They are a welcome sign of the spring to come and the expected rebirth of fertility.

December 6th SAINT NICHOLAS

December 6th is Saint Nicholas's Day. He was the original model for Santa Claus and much more is written about this fascinating character in a later chapter. It is on this day in Advent that many European children receive their gifts and special spiced biscuits known as SPECULAAS. This name comes from the Dutch word SPEK, meaning TIDBIT, and KLAAS, which is a shortened form of Nicholas. Godparents used to give delicious spiced honeybread to their godchildren on this day.

Often it is moulded into the shape of Bishop Nicholas rather like our gingerbread men. Because Nicholas was not only a bishop but also a patron saint of children, Boy Bishops used to be appointed at this time. An honour for the young boy concerned, but it also had its drawbacks as he had to preach a sermon. Not a task most small boys would look forward to! More of this fascinating custom is written about in the chapter dealing with Lords of Misrule.

RECIPE for SPECULAAS
(SAINT NICHOLAS'S DAY SPICED BISCUITS)

INGREDIENTS

8 oz	250g	Plain Flour
4 oz	125g	Soft brown sugar
4 oz	125g	Unsalted butter
1		Small egg

½ teaspoon each of powdered cloves, cardoman and cinnamon.

METHOD
a) Rub the butter into the flour
b) Cream the egg with the sugar and pour this into the flour and butter mixture

- c) Add the spices and mix together
- d) Leave the mixture to rest in a cool place for 20 minutes
- e) Roll the mixture out onto a floured board and cut into shapes or fingers about ½ inch thick

Bake at 350 F/180 C/ gas Mark 4 for approximately 10 minutes until golden brown.
When cool store in an air-tight box.
This amount makes some 20 delicious spiced biscuits.

December 13th SAINT LUCIA

December 13th is Saint Lucia's Day, one of the darkest days of winter. Saint Lucia, or Lucy, is celebrated with a festival of light which originated in far off pagan times when people practiced sympathetic magic to encourage the return of the warming sun to the earth. Nordic people believed that devils, witches and trolls were abroad at this time lurking in the darkness and they needed to be driven away with fire and lights.

Saint Lucia lived in Syracuse on the island of Sicily, sometime during the fourth century where she was murdered for her Christian beliefs. She is said to have carried food to the persecuted Christians who were hiding in the catacombs. She placed candles on her head, like the old miners of the past, so that her hands could be left free to carry provisions to the people hiding in the darkness of the underground burial places.

She is patroness of eye diseases. Again we see that darkness and light are involved. Often she is represented in pictures holding her two eyes in a dish, for she was cruelly blinded before being put to death. More is written about the Scandinavian ceremonies held on Saint Lucia's Day in Chapter 7 which deals with Candles, Lamps and Lanterns.

December 21st SAINT THOMAS

December 21st is Saint Thomas's Day, who is the patron saint of old people and probably because of this fact they were entitled to go "a Thomasing", which meant making the rounds of their local parish asking for alms. In some areas this custom went by the name of "mumping" or "going-a-gooding" for "goodenings". A little bag or collecting box was taken around to hold the coins and the "Thomasers" or "Mumpers" also carried a small basket containing evergreens, a sprig of which was given to everyone who contributed money. Carols were sung as the old people did their rounds and they were often wassail songs as the word means "good health" or "good cheer" and this constituted a yuletide greeting for every household visited.

Often children joined in this begging spree as one of our old carols illustrates:

> Here we come a' Thomasing
> all on this wintery night,
> We pray you of your charity
> to pity our sad plight.
> The night it is dark and the
> wind it is cold,
> We are the lame folk, the sick
> And the old.
> Here we come a' Thomasing
> knocking at your door,
> We pray you now good neighbours
> have pity on the poor.
> And Thomas he will bless you
> and all that dwell within,
> May the good God protect you
> and keep you free from sin.
>
> Anon

The cold, wet, unlit streets of olden times must indeed have been mirey or muddy to wander about in on a winter's night but no doubt the pennies collected by the young and aged parishioners made a very welcome addition to their meagre Christmas festivities. In very early times corn was often given instead of money so that the "Thomaser" had a good bag full of grain to make their bread with throughout the days of Christmastide.

In parts of the country trades-people gave small gifts to their regular customers on Goodening Day and this also happened until recent times on Boxing Day. Young unmarried girls believed that this was one of the special days of the year when it would be possible to foretell who their future husband was likely to be. They used to peel an onion just before they retired for the night and then stuck nine pins into it whilst reciting a special verse. After this was done she hoped to dream of her future spouse. With a large unpeeled onion next to her head on the pillow she probably awoke in tears!

CHRISTINGLES, CANDLES and CALENDARS

Customs come and go for tradition is not a static thing but changes and adapts with each succeeding generation. One of the newest of our customs is the Christingle Service, which is now held in churches throughout the land. It has become such an established Advent ceremony that it is hard to believe it only reached our shores in the late nineteen sixties. At that time the Children's Society adapted an old Moravian custom in order to raise funds for needy children and, at the same time, to give praise and thanks for God's love. The service appears to have been devised by a Moravian Pastor named John de Watterville, who lived in Marienborg, Germany. On December 20th 1747, he celebrated with the very first Christingle Service after which he asked the children present to take home the candles used and to re-light them every night until Christmas. Each house was encouraged to place a candle in the window to symbolise Christ's light shining out into the dark world outside.

Long before Pastor Watterville's day pagan people used to light candles and carry them around the streets at this time of the year, near to the winter solstice, to ward off evil. The candles or lanterns would be placed on the walls of a town surrounding it with light and thus forming a protective circle of flame. Maybe the Pastor knew about these old customs and adapted them to his own use.

Although the most popular period for Christingle celebrations falls between Advent and Epiphany, services may be held at anytime of the year, such as Easter and harvest time. These occasions, however, which involve dozens of glowing candles seem to call out for dark winter nights. Candlemas (February 2nd), would also be a most suitable date for it was on this day that the old medieval festival of Christmas ended and the blessing of candles to be used during the coming ecclesiastical year took place in churches and monasteries.

Christingle, Kriss Kringle or Krist Kindle means Christ's light and most people are now familiar with the oranges into which a lighted candle is placed and then presented to the congregation, especially the children. Long before Christingles reached our shores children in Wales used to carry CALLENIGS as they went around the streets singing their carols and collecting alms. In many ways these CALLENIGS, or Welsh Christmas apples, resembled Christingles for they consisted of an apple stuck all over with ears of corn which was surmounted by a sprig of berried holly. The apple was then mounted on three sticks by means of which it was carried around and afterwards stood on tables.

The fruit and corn obviously represent fruitfulness and plenty, holly was the ancient symbol of male fertility and also Christ's crown of thorns and everlasting life; possibly the three sticks came to represent the Holy Trinity. This is a very ancient custom and could date back to Celtic times when offerings of a similar nature were made to Brigid or Bridget, the Earth Mother, who was thought to protect crops and encourage healthy growth as had Ceres in the times of ancient Greece. It would be interesting to know if there is some connection between the European Kriss Kringle and the Celtic Callenig.

A Christingle

The Orange represents the world;
The candle symbolises God's light;
The red ribbon represents Christ's blood shed for mankind;
The four cocktail sticks show the seasons;
The fruits represent earth's fruitfulness.

ADVENT CROWNS

Another pretty custom which came to our shores in recent times, is the making of an Advent Crown or wreath. They are particularly popular in our churches, although many households also have them. In some ways they are similar to the old "Kissing Boughs" which used to decorate our homes over the Christmas period and these are described in a later chapter.

The wreath or "crown" consists of a circle of evergreens, such as ivy, holly, yew, bay etc. Into this ring of greenery is set four candles, one for each of the Advent Sundays which precede Christmas Eve. The first candle is lighted on Advent Sunday and then the others in turn on each succeeding Sunday until all four are alight. Sometimes a taller, larger candle, often of a contrasting colour, is set in the centre and this is lit on Christmas day. The candles symbolise the coming of light to the world with Christ, and the ring signifies God's love which is without beginning or end and which encircles and encompasses our lives. Advent wreaths are often hung from ceilings by coloured ribbons and look particularly festive in large buildings.

An Advent Crown

The practise of placing a wreath of evergreens on our front doors is also comparatively new to Britain. It is an American custom which seems to have caught-on in these islands after the Second World War (1939-1945). Hollywood may have inspired people to copy this custom as many films with Christmas themes showed these wreaths prominently displayed on homes in the snowy streets of American towns and cities. They certainly cheer up the drab winter scene encountered outside our houses during the run up to Christmas.

ADVENT CANDLES

These have also become popular in our homes and are marked off into twenty four sections with the first one being lit on December 1st and the last on Christmas Eve. Churches have specially made large Advent candles which are sectioned off into four parts and have a cross in the centre, often with the symbols for alpha and omega – the beginning and the end – on each side and these candles are lit during the Advent Services. Throughout Advent, light forms the most important part of celebrations.

ADVENT CALENDARS

Advent calendars did not form part of British celebrations until comparatively recent times. They were first seen here, in limited numbers, just after the Second World War in the 1950's. They seem to have originated in Germany or Austria during the late nineteenth century, the custom then crossed the Atlantic with emigrants moving to America and eventually they ended up on our shores. The custom very quickly caught on, being especially popular with young children, who love opening one small window on the calendar on each of the twenty four days preceding Christmas Day. Twenty three of the tiny pictures can depict anything of a seasonal or decorative nature but the twenty fourth, which is opened on Christmas Eve, always shows the Holy Family in the stable at Bethlehem.

Many modern versions have chocolates or small gifts concealed behind each window. It is very easy to make varying and original types of attractive Advent Calendars which can be used for many years afterwards. It is unfortunate that many modern Advent Calendars now depict tawdry and often horrific images such as monsters, dinosaurs, Barbie dolls and cartoon characters which have little, if anything, to do with the winter season or reflect the approaching Christmas festival.

Now the last window on our Advent Calendar has been opened and the Great Day has arrived!

It is quite a relief to relax on Christmas afternoon after this hectic four weeks of preparation. Much of this now has little to do with the spiritual preparations for the arrival of the Christ Child.

Commercialisation is the god which seems to dominate our modern Christmases. However, old traditions still survive and I hope you will enjoy reading about them, and their history, in the following chapters.

Advent Preparations

Sorry my dear, just can't stop,
Advent is here and it's time to shop;
Presents to buy in every store,
A wreath to collect for our front door;
And a bottle for "hubby" of really good wine.
There are cards to be bought of varied design,
Then written and posted in really good time.
A box of crackers is there on my list
Oh, and some lovely "choccies" I couldn't resist!
The pudding's to be made not to mention the cake,
The Turkey needs ordering - well, that can wait.
Gifts need selecting for distant relatives
After all this I'll be needing a sedative.
Well, time flies I must be on my way
But of course, my dear, I have to say
Is it really all worth it for just the one day?

Monica Evans

Now we Merthe

Now we merthe al and sum,
For Christmasse now is i com!

Now make we mery bothe more and las,
For now is the time of Crist mas.

Now everyman at my request
Be glad and mery all in this fest.

Lett no man cum into this hall,
Grome, page, nor yet marshall;
But that sum sport he bryng withall;
For now is the time of Cristymas!

If he say he can nowght do,
Then for my love aske hym no mo,
But to the stokkis then lett hym go,
For now is the time of Cristymas!

Medieval Poem Anon 14th C

2

CHRISTMAS

Man, be glad in halle and hour;
This tyme was born our savyour.
Make we myrth,
For Criste's byrth.

Anon   14th century

Our present Christmas or "Christ's Mass" celebrations evolve from the religious celebration of the Christ Child's birth in Bethlehem. Long before this date, however, pagan festivities and rites were celebrated during the month of December throughout Europe. At this, the coldest and darkest part of the year, festivals of light and rejoicing were held.

The Roman Saturnalia was celebrated from December 17th until December 24th in honour of Saturn, the god of agriculture. It, in turn, sprang from fertility customs and rites practised in ancient times around the Mediterranean area to placate the earth gods and also to promote fertility in man, beast and crops. They also prayed for the return of the sun in springtime to warm the earth and make it productive again. These were the earliest fire festivals which pre-date our Christmas by thousands of years but which clearly form the basis of many of our customs. Saturnalia was a wild festival, when buildings were lit up with torches and lamps and decorated with evergreens, also presents and greetings were exchanged amongst friends, relatives and neighbours. Men dressed up as animals and women (a tradition still to be observed in our pantomimes), everyone wore masks which were both grotesque and comical, slaves were, temporarily, equals of their masters who waited on them during the festivities. We see echoes of this exchanging of the master/slave roles today when officers in the armed forces serve the lower ranks on Christmas Day with their annual Christmas dinner. Kindly Saturn ruled the world of Rome for these few winter days.

Lucian, a Greek, writing in the days of ancient Rome during the third century said:

"It (Saturnalia) is marked by drinking, being drunk, noise, games, dance, feasting of slaves, singing naked, appointing mock kings, and an occasional ducking of corked faces in icy water. All business, be it private or public, is forbidden during the feast days save such as tend to sport, solace and delight. Let none follow their avocations except cooks and bakers."

The poor old cooks, be they housewives or employed chefs, never seem to get a rest.

He went on to say that:

"All men shall be equal, slave and free, rich and poor, one with another."

On December 25th, the Birthday of the Unconquered Sun, or Brumalia, took place in Roman times. This was a festival in honour of Mithras, the Persian God of the Sun, whose cult had been introduced by the Legions serving in that country. Mithraism has many teachings in common with Christianity and at one time was seen as its great rival.

Oblations were offered up entreating the kindly sun to return to earth during the forthcoming spring and bring not only new life to the earth but enlightenment to mens' hearts. It too was concerned with brotherly love, fellowship, and the bringing of light to the world. Women, however, were excluded from the cult, it being an all male religion particularly popular with the Roman legions.

This was the winter solstice when the sun was, and is, farthest away from the northern hemisphere. December is, throughout Europe, one of the coldest, darkest and most dreary times of year. Festivals of light and hope were necessary to help ancient peoples through the long winter. Christmas gives us the same lifting of spirits even today. It is something to look forward to and enjoy when there is little else to entertain our thoughts.

We must remember that our ancestors did not enjoy the holidays we have today. Christmas or Yule was the only break from work for more than a few days in the whole of their working year. It also happened to coincide with the period when work became more or less impossible on the frozen or waterlogged land. Landowners were crafty enough to encourage the holiday to be taken when it would not cause themselves any loss or inconvenience. In spite of this, it was a time much looked forward to by poor people as the only great feast of the year which was contributed to by their master, (though some did hold a harvest supper for workers and tenants in early autumn, but this was just an evening's entertainment as compared to the longer period of the Christmas, Yule or Saturnalian celebrations).

On January 1st, the Juvenalia, or Feast of the Children, took place throughout the Roman Empire. This was much looked forward to by the young Romans, as gifts were given to them, and special parties and events were held in their honour. There is a strong link here with our present day Christmas.

The feast of the Kalends (Kalendae Januarii) was also held on this, the first day of the New Year. It was dedicated to the god Janus with his two-sided head. One of his faces looked back into the old year, and one faced forward towards the coming year. Our word "calendar" comes from this festival. All of these festivals were well established long before Christ was born. Many people believe that

December 25th was actually Christ's birthday, but this is not correct. The actual date is unknown and will probably always remain so.

The early Christian fathers, or leaders, chose this date on which to celebrate his birth because of the existing celebrations taking place at this time. In their wisdom they decided to compromise with existing customs in order to encourage membership of the church. Christian festivals overlapped the heathen ones on purpose, for it was easier to rename a festival than to ban it entirely, thus driving it underground, or to invent new and unfamiliar holidays or "holy days". A compromise with existing customs encouraged membership of the newly formed Christian church. New adherents to the faith did not want to miss out on all the fun taking place at various times through the year. General Booth, of the Salvation Army once said "Why should the Devil have all the best tunes?" The first Christian leaders must have thought along similar lines, i.e., why should the pagans have all the best festivals?

Not all the churches agreed about the date for Christmas. The Eastern church chose to celebrate on January 5th and 6th, and it still adheres to these dates. The Russian Orthodox church celebrates the occasion on January 7th.

So the Birthday celebrations of the Unconquered Sun on December 25th became the Birthday of the Son of Righteousness. Christ is often referred to by this title, and Christians still refer to Him as being "The Light of the World". There are obvious links with former pagan worship in these titles.

Ambrose, Bishop of Milan from 339 - 397 A.D. said:

"Well do Christian people call this holy day on which our Lord was born the Day of the New Sun".

A new slant and emphasis had been put on the old Festivals of the Sun. The Nativity was first officially celebrated in Rome on December 25th in 354 A.D.

The Vikings and Norsemen also held a great festival of fire during December. Bonfires were lit and torches were carried during outdoor rites, and many lights illuminated the interiors of the great halls. These festivals were, like the Roman ones, all to do with encouraging the sun to return and bring fertility during the coming year. This Norse festival was Yule, a word still used by us, hence Yule-log, Yuletide greetings, etc. Jul remains the word for Christmas in Scandinavia. Fire was thought to discourage evil spirits lurking in the winter gloom and darkness, also it refined and purified the earth. The brightness and warmth of a glowing fire or flame gave comfort and security during the cold darkness of a northern winter. It is understandable that fire should become the symbol of hope.

December 25th was the beginning of the Anglo Saxon year and the time when the Yuletide festivities began. Christmas was first celebrated on any scale in England with the arrival of St. Augustine in 592 A.D., although small groups of Christians up and down the British Isles, who were converted by the early Roman and Celtic missionaries, probably observed this day before Augustine's arrival. According to the Venerable Bede, writing during the eighth century, Yule was preceded by Modranicht, or the Night of the Mothers - another parallel with the cult of the Virgin perhaps?. At this time the Saxons kept watch and performed religious ceremonies in honour of the Earth Mother goddess.

On Christmas Day in 598 A.D. Saint Augustine baptised 10,000 Anglo-Saxon converts. That must have been a chilly occasion for all concerned as, in those days, it was usually done by total immersion in a nearby river or stream.

King Alfred was a keen observer of Christmas and its festivities. He enforced the keeping of the Twelve Days of Christmas between the Nativity and Epiphany, January 6th, in accordance with the law of the church. During those twelve days no work was supposed to be done, legal proceedings were suspended, and all people were commanded to live in "accord and love". It is said that Alfred carried his principles into practice so far that he lost the battle of Chippenham against the Danes in 878 A.D. because he refused to fight during the Twelve Days of Christmas, which were so revered by him.

King Edward the Confessor ordained it to be a "holy tide of peace and concord" in his laws compiled during the eleventh century. Although the Saxons were Christian to a greater extent during the ninth, tenth and eleventh centuries, paganism lingered on in peoples' minds. Old customs died hard - they appeared as an "insurance" a belt and braces policy for extra protection against disaster. We must remember that the word pagan (paganus in Latin) originally meant "country dweller", likewise "heathen" meant a person who dwelt on heathlands. They were nature worshippers concerned with the fertility of the earth and all growing things which were bound up with the agricultural cycle each year. Their gods were deities of the natural world so important to them all for keeping life going. They were not "Satanists" or evil people given up to wicked and lustful pursuits as many people imagine. Their old religion, like Christianity, had rules, teachings, and strict codes of conduct. It was not as difficult as people imagine for paganism in its truest sense to exist side by side with Christianity. We can see now how the ancient customs observed by our long distant ancestors became so entwined with Christian festivals that they were still being carried on in Medieval times, though their origins were forgotten. These customs have been passed down, through the centuries, to us in modern times.

People today enjoy putting up the holly, lighting their candles, decorating their trees, feasting and drinking, although many are not quite sure why they continue with these traditions. We see that our present day Christmas is an amalgam of pagan and Christian rites, ancient and relatively new customs, feasting, carousing and worship, a time for goodwill towards ones neighbours, servants and even enemies, of gift giving, and a resting time from the grind of everyday chores and work.

In our modern day Christmas celebrations it is almost impossible to disentangle fact from legend or the pagan from the Christian aspects. It has all become a rich mixture of superstition, religion and general enjoyment. As may be seen, it goes back much further into our past than most people imagine. Most of the customs which we observe at this time of year have stories and legends woven around them. Their history is a fascinating one which links us in a very tangible way to our ancestors' past enjoyment of the Yuletide season.

Christmas Thoughts

Amidst the holly and tinsel and all the Christmas joy,
Let us pause, for just a moment, and remember the birth of a boy
Who lay amongst the cattle and was content to be there.
Our God, transformed to manhood, who took our sin and care.
There was no Christmas feasting upon that holy day,
Just warmth in a primitive cow shed and a little prickly hay.
There was no Christmas stocking, all packed with gaudy things
Instead, the symbols of his passion brought by distant kings,
No tree full of lights and gaily wrapped presents to share
But a group of poor local shepherds kneeling in silent prayer.
No candles shining in the dark with warm and comforting glow,
Only a great and glorious star reflected on the snow:
No cosy room with paper chains festooned on every wall
Just Mary and her baby who is the God of all.

Monica Evans

"Make we merry……"

3

GREEN GROW'TH THE HOLLY

*Green grow'th the holly,
So doth the ivy;
Though winter blasts blow ne'er so high,
Green grow'th the holly.*

*As the holly grow'th free and never changeth hue,
So I have now and ever been unto my lady true.
Green grow'th the holly etc.*

*As the holly grow'th free with ivy all alone
When flowers cannot be seen and green wood trees be gone,
Green grow'th the holly etc.*

(Part of the song attributed to
Henry VIII. Circa 1515.)

HOLLY

The holly, or "holy" tree, was once held to be so powerful and sacred that it was planted in gardens to ward off evil and deter witches from crossing the threshold of a house. That is why so many ancient holly trees are to be found in the gardens of country houses and cottages. Country people in the past were very superstitious about such things.

Holly, with its dark green, glossy leaves and brilliant scarlet berries, has been used for thousands of years for winter decoration. We can understand why for it shows up brightly against the wintery landscape, and it lasts for long periods of time when put into decorations. If holly is kept damp and cool it will not dry up for weeks on end. It often seems to be so strongly linked to our modern Christmas that we fail to realise that the Romans used it in much the same way as we do today. It was hung in branches or bunches outside their wineshops and inns, instead of our familiar pub signs, to denote the fact that wine was on sale within its walls, for holly was sacred to Bacchus, the ancient god of the vine. Inns in those days were often small places with little else to distinguish them from the surrounding buildings. "The Holly Bush" remains a popular name for pubs in these modern times.

Holly was the symbol of everlasting life because it did not appear to die off in autumn like other trees, or to shed its leaves. In ancient times it was felt that the gods and goddesses of fertility left the earth during the autumn when the flowers and fruits of the earth disappeared, plants withered and the leaves of trees fell down to the ground with the onset of winter. All living plants appeared to die except for the evergreen shrubs and trees such as the holly, yew, mistletoe, fir trees, ivy etc: and so primitive man assumed that the gods of nature went to dwell in those evergreens until the coming of spring.

During the winter solstice they were taken into the pagan temples and places of worship much as we place them in our churches today. This denoted reverence for the gods and goddesses of the earth. The evergreen swags and wreaths denoted everlasting life, especially the wreaths, for the circle is a symbol of time without beginning and without end and has always had mystical and symbolic associations. Even our wedding rings symbolise an unbroken love, although this often fails to live up to early expectations.

In olden days hedgers were very wary about cutting down a holly tree growing amongst the other hedging shrubs and trees during the annual hedging and ditching tidy up. Often the holly was left growing up through the hedge to form a strong tree. Many of these can still be seen in our countryside. Tree worship has always been at the back of country peoples' minds and it still causes pain to many people to see trees cut down. Our ancestors felt it could bring down the wrath of the gods upon them and their families.

Like many other things to do with our Christmas customs, holly was originally pagan but became Christianised. As a plant it held the symbols of Christ's Passion. The leaves grow out from the stem on alternate sides forming cruciform patterns, and their sharp, piercing, prickly spikes denote the crown of thorns which Christ wore during His Crucifixion. The brilliant scarlet berries symbolise the blood which flowed from His head, hands and feet. There are several legends surrounding the holly, and one goes as follows:

Once the berries growing on the holly tree were not the scarlet colour which we know today, but were pale green like those we see on the tree before its berries have ripened. When Christ was taken out to be scourged and crucified His crown of thorns was formed by branches of intertwined holly. As the droplets of blood fell down from his pierced brow they touched the then green berries turning them red. The holly tree has had blood red berries ever since that day. It may be seen that this little story also serves to Christianise the plant, and probably superseded some of the earlier tales.

The Holly and the Ivy

The holly and the ivy
Now both are full grown
Of all the trees that are in the wood,
The Holly bears the crown.

Chorus: *The rising of the sun*
And the running of the deer,
The playing of the merry organ,
Sweet singing in the choir.

The holly bears a blossom
As white as any flower,
And Mary bore sweet Jesus Christ
To be our sweet Saviour.

Chorus

The holly bears a berry
As red as any blood,
And Mary bore sweet Jesus Christ
To do poor sinners good.

Chorus

The holly bears a prickle
As sharp as any thorn,
And Mary bore sweet Jesus Christ
On Christmas Day in the morn.

Chorus

(Traditional)

This familiar carol bears elements of Christian and pagan worship, for it follows the events of Christ's birth and death in its verses, whilst the chorus appears to contain pagan symbolism, i.e. the rising sun and the ritual pursuit of an animal. It is possible that this carol was adapted from an old song long lost in the mists of time. The holly is said to represent the male side of fertility and "bears the crown", an ancient male prerogative, whilst the ivy represents the female side, perhaps because it clings, is long lasting, hard to get rid of and tenacious in habit! It is also pliable but extremely tough. Holly, like the male species, is prickly, tough and hard to handle. Not unsuitable analogies really!

In the olden days holly and other evergreens were put behind pictures, along the mantlepiece above the fireplace and around candlesticks.

John Clare, the humble Northamptonshire farm worker, who became a well-known poet during the nineteenth century, wrote in his poem "The Shepherd's Calendar" a description of a poor man's Christmas about two hundred years ago. Evergreens certainly had an important role in the decoration of even the most unpretentious cottages, as can be seen in this extract from his poem.

> *Christmass is come and every hearth*
> *Makes room to give him welcome now*
> *E'en want will dry its tears in mirth*
> *And crown him wi' a holly bough*
> *Tho' tramping 'neath a winter's sky*
> *O'er snowy track paths and rhymey stiles*
> *The huswife sets her spinning bye*
> *And bids him welcome wi' her smiles*
>
> *Each house is swept the day before*
> *And windows stuck wi' evergreens*
> *The snow is beesom'd from the door*
> *And comfort crowns the cottage scenes*
> *Gilt holly wi' its thorny pricks*
> *And yew and box wi' berrys small*
> *These deck the unus'd candlesticks*
> *And pictures hanging by the wall*

After the Christmas celebrations are over and the decorations taken down on Twelfth Night, the evergreens should never be thrown out onto a rubbish heap, or suffer the indignity of being placed in a dustbin. They should be burnt at the end of the Yuletide festivities, for they are sacred plants and must, by tradition, only be consumed by the sacred element of fire. It is said to bring bad luck to any household if this custom is not observed. The old gods object to being rammed down with a lot of miscellaneous rubbish. If you happen to live in the middle of a city with only central heating and no fireplace in your house or flat I think you have problems!

Holly certainly makes a marvellous blaze, for it is full of natural volatile oils also it scents a room with a sweet smokey odour whilst it crackles away in the hearth.

The berries on our holly trees provide much needed food for the birds in a hard winter, but they are not their favourite food as the berries are bitter and are only resorted to when all other food is unavailable.

Nowadays we see holly printed on almost anything to do with Christmas, from wrapping paper to toilet rolls. Little do most people realise its ancient significance.

Unfortunately, many people resort to putting up plastic variations of this lovely tree. Far better to use real evergreens such as ivy or yew if holly is difficult to obtain. We can be sure that no god ever deigned to dwell in a synthetic substitute, except perhaps the god of commerce and a thousand tinkling cash tills.

4

MISTLETOE

"This amorous spray….."

Come Kiss Me, or the Lost Opportunity

Come kiss me under the mistletoe,
Come kiss me and I'll let you go.

Come kiss me under its pearly berries,
Press close to mine your lips like cherries.

Come kiss me, for what girl can resist
By such a fine fellow to be kissed.

Come kiss me! I'll add you to the list
Of all the willing girls I've kissed.

Come kiss me, no you must not frown.
No woman to date has turned me down.
Come kiss me under this amorous spray.
Well, I'll be damned, she's walked away!

                              Monica Evans

Mistletoe was the most sacred of plants to our pagan forbears. It is the Golden Bough of ancient mythology steeped in legend and mystical uses. The cut boughs of mistletoe assume a rich golden ochre colour as they dry out and probably this accounts for its ancient name.

It was especially sacred to the Druids in Celtic Britain and only the High Priest or Arch Druid was allowed to cut a branch of this most sacred plant during the winter solstice ceremonies. Mistletoe has always been connected with its host tree the oak, and the word "druid" means "oak-man". So sacred was this plant that no ordinary sickle of iron was used during the ceremonies but instead one made of pure gold which was reserved for the use of the Arch Druid.

During the Roman occupation of Britain these customs were observed and written about by the occupying forces. Pliny writes:

"The Druids, for so they call their wizards, esteem nothing more sacred than the mistletoe and the tree on which it grows, provided only that the tree is oak. But apart from this they choose oak-woods for their sacred groves and perform no sacred rites without oak-leaves; so that the very name of "Druid" may be regarded as a Greek appellation derived from their worship of the oak.

They believe that whatever grows on these trees is sent from heaven, and is a sign that the tree has been chosen by the god himself. The mistletoe is very rarely to be met with; but when it is found, they gather it with solemn ceremony. This they do above all on the sixth day of the moon, from whence they date the beginnings of their months, of their years, and of their thirty years cycle, because by the sixth day the moon has plenty of vigour and has not run half its course. After due preparations have been made for a sacrifice and a feast under the tree, they hail it as the universal healer and bring to the spot two white bulls, whose horns have never been bound before. A priest clad in a white robe climbs the tree and with a golden sickle cuts the mistletoe, which is caught in a white cloth. They sacrifice the victims, praying that God may make his own gift to prosper with those upon whom he has bestowed it. They believe that a potion prepared from the mistletoe will make barren animals to bring forth, and the plant is a remedy against all poison."

It will be seen from this passage that the mistletoe was not allowed to touch the earth, being caught in a white cloth held by virgins as it fell from the host tree, and it is still deemed unlucky for it to come into contact with the ground. Probably this stemmed from the belief that the plant embodied the god and contact with the floor or soil would cause pollution and call down the wrath from heaven.

The winter solstice ceremonies took place throughout northern Europe (in Celtic times) during the month of December, usually between the 20th and the 22nd day of that month, a date not far removed from our own Christmastide.

In the Greek and Roman world a piece of mistletoe used to be worn to denote a time of truce during the solstice celebrations. The two separate but conjoined leaves of the mistletoe plant are a telling symbol of unity. Vendettas and thoughts of war and violence towards ones' enemies were supposed to be set aside at this time.

The mistletoe plant is also symbolic of male fertility, and the pearly white berries with their sticky juice were equated with the life giving male semen. Ancient peoples also believed that the plant contained the seminal fluid flowing from the god through the host oak tree. This relatively insignificant parasitic growth held all the mystery of fertility and rebirth to our ancestors. They also noted that the mistletoe remained green and full of life whilst the host tree shed its leaves and appeared to die during the winter months. The life of the oak appeared to transfer itself into the mistletoe bough at this time of year.

Even today this plant is somewhat scarce and it is exciting to find it growing on host trees of apple, hawthorn or oak, where it is mostly planted by mistle thrushes when they wipe the sticky seeds from their beaks on the rough bark after enjoying a wintery meal from its berries.

Like many evergreens it grows only slowly and is difficult to propagate by hand. Mistletoe is mostly found in the West Country but it also thrives in the apple orchards of Normandy and Brittany.

Much of the mistletoe we buy at Christmas is now imported from France, although mistletoe auctions take place in England's west country during early December.

But why, you may ask, do we kiss under mistletoe and always place it high up in the air? The following Norse legend may help to explain matters.

Long ago in Asgard, the dwelling place of the Norse gods, there lived a handsome and good god named Balder the Bright and Beautiful. He was the Viking god of the sun who was greatly loved by all the other gods of Asgard except for one named Loki. Now Frigg, his mother, who was also queen of Asgard, loved Balder so greatly that she made all things upon earth promise never to harm him.

All plants, trees, metals, rocks, stones, animals, birds, all creeping creatures, even the sacred elements of earth, fire and water, were made to promise never to injure him in any way. Now, only one plant was overlooked and this was the mistletoe which at this time was a lowly plant growing amongst the roots of a great tree. Frigg failed to notice this insignificant plant, but the evil god Loki had not!

Because it was known that nothing could harm Balder, the young gods of Asgard made sport with him, hurling missiles of stone, iron and wood at his body. They all bounced harmlessly off the smiling Balder. Now Balder had a blind brother named Hoder and he longed to join in with the laughter and high spirited games of his companions but his blindness prevented him from doing so.

Loki, the evil one, decided to use both Hoder and the mistletoe to bring about Balder's downfall. He took a thick stake of the mistletoe branch and sharpened it to a point, afterwards hardening it in fire until he had a short but strong spear. Loki then asked Hoder if he would like to join in the games with the other young gods. Of course he replied in the affirmative and the wicked Loki placed the spear in Hoder's hand, guided his aim and the spear shot forward piercing Balder's heart and killing him.

Great was the sorrow and lamentation in Asgard when the news broke. Balder's body was placed in a long-boat which was set on fire and pushed blazing out to sea by the giantess Hyrrokim. Frigg caused Loki to be driven out of Asgard and the mistletoe was cursed for eternity and forced to grow high up on the oak as a hated parasite and forbidden to touch earth ever again.

Since that time a kiss beneath a bunch or sprig of mistletoe has denoted love to the recipient in memory of the beautiful and beloved Balder. The same kiss also acted as a charm against harm from the elements of earth, fire and water. It has, since pagan days, remained a symbol of sexual love and fertility.

The mistletoe's early pagan associations are evident and it was forbidden by the Church as a decoration at Christmas. The Puritans in seventeenth century England saw it as a pernicious and ungodly plant and banned its use completely during the years of Cromwell's rule - indeed the entire festival of Christmas, both secular and religious, was abolished during the eleven years of the Commonwealth, only being reinstated with the return of Charles II to the throne in 1660.

The only church in England where mistletoe is allowed to take a place in the Christmas ceremonies is York Minster, where sprays are placed on a salver and presented at the altar, presumably thus sanctifying the plant.

During a visit to England in 1815 Washington Irving, an American, recorded his impressions of an English Christmas in his *"Sketch Book"*, first published in 1875. He observed the following incident concerning mistletoe:

"On reaching the church porch we found the parson rebuking the grey-headed sexton for having used mistletoe among the greens with which the church was decorated. It was, he observed, an unholy plant, profaned by having been used by the Druids in their mystic ceremonies; and though it might be innocently employed in the festive ornamenting of halls and kitchens, yet it had been deemed by Fathers of the Church as unhallowed, and totally unfit for sacred purposes. So tenacious was he on this point that the poor sexton was obliged to strip down a great part of the humble trophies of his taste before the parson would consent to enter upon the service of the day."

In an additional note he adds:

"The mistletoe is still hung up in farmhouses and kitchens at Christmas; and the young men have the privilege of kissing the girls under it, plucking each time a berry from the bush. When the berries are all plucked the privilege ceases."

Until quite recently great circular kissing boughs or rings were hung from the beams of mansions, farms and even humble cottages. They were patently a fertility symbol with the outer ring made of entwined holly, yew and ivy, pierced through the centre with a large bunch of mistletoe. Apples were hung from it denoting fruitfulness and fecundity, and four candles were placed on the outer circle to represent the four seasons and, in early times, the returning light of the life giving sun and later on in Christian times, they symbolised the coming of light to the world with the birth of Jesus Christ.

Long before the Christmas tree ever came to these islands the kissing bough was the principal decoration in our ancestor's homes at Christmastide or Yule. Kisses exchanged by lovers under this bough naturally imply not only love but also fertility. After each kiss a berry should be removed until there are none left. No berries, no kisses!

John Clare observed this rural custom in his poem, "The Shepherd's Calendar" written in the 1820's.

> *The shepherd now no more afraid*
> *Since custom doth the chance bestow*
> *Starts up to kiss the giggling maid*
> *Beneath the branch of mizzletoe*
> *That 'neath each cottage beam is seen*
> *Wi' pearl-like berrys shining gay*
> *The shadow still of what hath been*
> *Which fashion yearly fades away.*

Mistletoe, like holly, should never be discarded casually or thrown into a rubbish bin, instead it must be burnt. Not only was mistletoe a decorative and mystical plant but it was, and still is, a valuable plant used in medicines and cosmetics. It is, however, a potent and poisonous plant which contains viscotoxin and over seventeen differing amino acids. In the past it was used to cure nervous disorders, convulsions, delirium, neuralgia and diseases of the heart.

The Druids used it to cure epilepsy and infertility. It was also believed that they used it to induce a trance-like hallucigenic state of mind during special ceremonies. Too much of its toxic constituents very likely made them exceedingly sick or very dead!

Cosmetically, mistletoe has many uses being an excellent ingredient in soothing face creams. In Lotion form it is an effective astringent for correcting greasy skin conditions and open pores. Many anti-dandruff shampoos contain extract of mistletoe. Homeopathy still finds a place for this ancient plant among its cures. It has come down the centuries to us retaining much of its old mystery and power.

Like everything else to do with Christmas there is more to the mistletoe plant than most people could imagine.

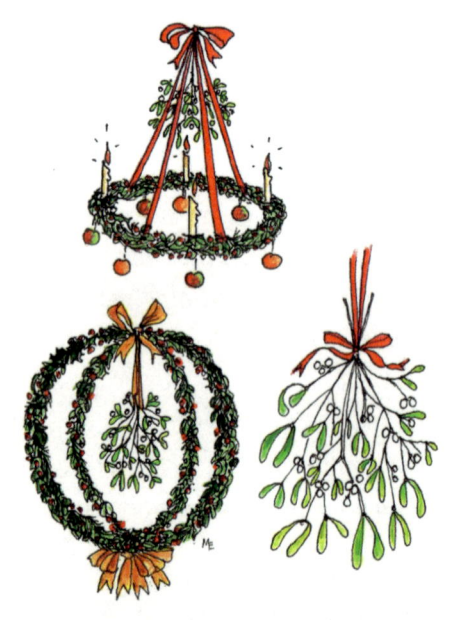

Some examples of kissing boughs

5

FATHER CHRISTMAS
or
SANTA CLAUS ?

He was dressed all in fur, from his head to his foot,
And his clothes were all tarnished with ashes and soot;
A bundle of toys he had flung on his back,
And he looked like a pedlar just opening his pack.

A Visit from St Nicholas,
Clement C.Moore. 1823.

Santa Claus

He comes in the night! He comes in the night!
He softly, silently comes;
While the little brown heads on the pillows so white
Are dreaming of bugles and drums.
He cuts through the snow like a ship through the foam,
While the white flakes around him whirl;
Who tells him I know not, but he findeth the home
Of each good little boy and girl.

His sleigh it is long, and deep, and wide,
It will carry a host of things.
While dozens of drums hang over the side,
With sticks sticking under the strings.
And yet not the sound of a drum is heard,
Not a bugle blast is blown,
As he mounts to the chimney-top like a bird,
And drops to the hearth like a stone.

The little red stockings he silently fills,
Till the stockings will hold no more;
The bright little sleds for the great snow hills
Are quickly set down on the floor.
Then Santa Claus mounts to the roof like a bird,
And glides to his seat in the sleigh;
Not the sound of a bugle or drum is heard
As he noiselessly gallops away.

He rides to the East, and he rides to the West.
Of his goodies he touches not one;
He eateth the crumbs of the Christmas feast
When the dear little folks are done.
Old Santa Claus doeth all he can;
This beautiful mission is his;
Then children, be good to this little old man
When you find who the little man is.

Anon.

Ask a child what it most likes about Christmas and I think the answer would be, "Father Christmas and presents". Like everything else connected with Christmas his origins are both obscure and complicated; a mixture of fact and fiction.

The original Father Christmas or Santa Claus was Saint Nicholas, a holy man born around about 270 A.D. in the town of Patara, which is now part of present day Turkey. He was saintly even as a child, and legend says he prayed with tiny hands held together whilst still an infant in arms. Another old tradition tells how he refused to suckle at his mother's breast on fast days.

A difficult child one can imagine!

He became a priest on reaching manhood and eventually he was made Bishop of Myra, then part of Asia Minor, and now in modern day Turkey. By all accounts he was as kindly and thoughtful as he was holy. He cared about all the people in his flock and he was always ready to help any of them whenever they were in need. Evidently he was much loved by the poor people of his diocese for his generosity and kindness. There are many legends which tell of his Christian acts of charity. Christianity was, however, not wholly accepted by the Roman Empire at this date and he was eventually martyred for his Christian faith during the reign of Diocletian in about 340 A.D.

The fat, jolly, red-coated old man is a comparatively new image of Father Christmas or Santa Claus, and it reflects the worldly, hedonistic figures of Saturn, much in evidence during the Roman Saturnalia, and also the all powerful Odin worshipped at Yule by the ancient Norse peoples.

In 1616 Ben Jonson described the seventeenth century idea of the figure Christmas in his "Masque for Christmas" written for the court of James I. Father Christmas is described as follows ...

"...enter Christmas with two or three of the Guard, attired in round hose, long stockings, a close doublet, a high-crowned hat with a brooch, a long thin beard, a truncheon, little ruffes, white shoos, his scarfes and garters tied cross, and his drum beaten before him."

... not at all like our familiar, modern style Santa Claus.

In England, right up to Victorian times, he was often referred to as Old Father Winter. He wore a long green gown trimmed with fur, green being the magical colour of fertility, also a wreath of holly and other evergreens, such as ivy and yew, crowned his flowing white hair. Charles Dickens describes the character of Christmas Present as being so attired in his story "A Christmas Carol".

A Green Father Christmas as depicted on a late 19th century Christmas card

In his hand, Old Father Christmas, sometimes carried a wassail bowl; frequently he was depicted as being surrounded by wine goblets and bottles. He was a bibulous and worldly figure owing more to Bacchus than the saintly Nicholas. The ancient Norsemen believed that Odin, their chief god, roamed the world during the Yuletide period in the guise of a bearded old man, distributing gifts to the worthy.

"Santa Claus" was not a universally recognized figure in Britain until the late nineteenth century as the following letter, written in 1879 to the Folklore Society, would seem to confirm.

"Sirs,

I have not seen the following observance recorded anywhere and having been only lately told of it by a country person cognizant of its observance both in Herefordshire and Worcestershire from personal knowledge reaching up to last year perhaps in addition to other folk lore it may be worth a place in Notes and Queries". On Christmas Eve, when the inmates of the house in the country retire to bed, all those desirous of a present, place a stocking outside the door of their bedroom, with the expectation that some mythical being called Santiclaus will fill the stocking or place something within it before the morning. This is of course well known and the master of the house does in reality place a Christmas gift secretly in each stocking; but the giggling girls in the morning, when bringing down their presents, affect to say that Santiclaus visited and filled the stockings in the night. From what region of the earth or air this benevolent Santiclaus takes flight I have not been able to ascertain but probably he may be heard of in other countries than those I have mentioned. An Exeter resident tells me this custom prevails also in Devonshire".

How, then, did all these various figures from the past become the Santa Claus which we know today? The answer is that he is an American invention which, in turn arose from the figure of Sinterklaas taken across the Atlantic by early Dutch settlers. We can see how the name of Santa Claus is derived - San Nicholas - Sinterklaas - Santa Claus.

In Holland Sinterklaas arrives on Saint Nicholas's feast day, December 6th. He is dressed in a Bishop's robe and mitre, not the more recent familiar garb of red with white fur. He rides a white horse and is accompanied by a black-faced Moorish helper named Piet, who carries a bundle of birches with which to beat naughty children. Piet was originally a Spanish figure and it would seem that his appearance dates from the Spanish occupation of the Netherlands in the sixteenth century.

In towns all over Holland these two figures appear on December 6th, Saint Nicholas's Feast Day, much to the joy of watching and expectant children. No doubt they take careful note of the large sack containing toys which is slung across the back of the horse.

> Put your long red mantle on,
> Saint Nicholas, good holy man!
> Drive your sleigh from Amsterdam,
> And find us quickly as you can.

(An old Dutch rhyme.)

After a day of feasting and games the Dutch children place a shoe by the fire containing hay and a juicy carrot for Sinterklaas' horse. Next morning they hope to find a present in the shoe left by the splendid figure of Bishop Nicholas. In the past naughty children, could expect a beating from Black Piet. This is an interesting variant on the traditional arrival of our Father Christmas on Christmas Eve. But why, you may question, do we hang up stockings? Again the answer is provided by an old legend connected with the original Saint Nicholas.

In the town of Myra, where Nicholas was bishop, lived a poor man with three young and marriageable daughters. Now in those days a dowry of a considerable sum of money was required before a girl could obtain a suitable husband. This poor man could not raise enough money to endow even one of his daughters let alone the other two! So he decided that the only way open to him was to sell them into slavery, (some versions say prostitution). Now Saint Nicholas heard about their plight, and one night, under cover of darkness, he crept up to the man's open window and threw in a bag of gold which landed in a stocking hanging up to dry above the fireplace (other accounts of this story say it landed in a shoe). The poor man was delighted and his eldest daughter was duly married and settled.

A little while elapsed, and on one dark night a second bag of gold came through the window.

The second daughter was then able to make a good marriage. Of course the poor man was curious to find out who was the generous donor of these gifts, so he determined to remain awake by his fire every night in the hope that a third bag of gold would be thrown through his window. Maybe, he thought, he would catch a glimpse of the generous donor. Sure enough, a few nights later a third purse of gold was tossed through the window and the poor man was just in time to catch a glimpse of the face belonging to their own beloved Bishop Nicholas before it disappeared into the darkness of the night. He told his friends and neighbours of Saint Nicholas' kindness and the story was passed down from father to son.

Now we can see how the stockings and shoes placed by our fireplaces on Christmas Eve have become part of the complicated pattern of our Christmas traditions. Saint Nicholas became the patron saint of children because he was said to have brought to life three little boys murdered by an innkeeper, a Sweeney Todd of his day, who pickled them in brine in readiness for making them into dishes for his customers. Besides this he is the patron saint of sailors because he caused a violent storm at sea to abate whilst journeying on a pilgrimage to the Holy Land thus saving the lives of the terrified crew.

Nicholas is also the patron of pawnbrokers and thieves perhaps the two were synonymous to the medieval mind! This is because the wealthy Medici family, who became some of the earliest and most successful bankers in Europe during the sixteenth century, took the three bags of gold as their badge.

These bags of gold hung above their banking houses as a badge or trade mark. Gradually the shape became simplified to the three golden balls we are familiar with today.

Eventually not only bankers but also pawnbrokers and money-lenders used this familiar symbol to denote their trade. During the Middle Ages, Saint Nicholas was one of Europe's most popular saints and hundreds of churches were dedicated to him. He is patron saint of Russia, Greece and Amsterdam.

The jolly red-coated figure of Santa Claus (Sinterklass) crossed the Atlantic sometime during the nineteenth century and gradually merged with our own Father Christmas, who, in turn, evolved from pagan mythical figures as well as Saint Nicholas himself.

Santa's pointed hood or hat and short red tunic would seem to owe much in style to the Icelandic Jola Sveinar, the Swedish Jultomten and the Norwegian and Danish Julnisse, these little red clad elves appeared bearing gifts and bringing blessings to a household during the Jul celebrations. It is interesting to note that the word nisse is an old Scandinavian form of the name Nicholas. It would seem that immigrants from Scandinavia, settling in America, played a part in the style of clothing finally decided upon for Santa Claus. This round, cheery figure of Santa had great appeal for many American commercial interests who used his jovial character in their various advertising campaigns.

Coca-Cola, whose trade name was in red and white, seized the opportunity to publicise their drink on posters and in magazine advertisements by depicting red coated, jolly old Santa enjoying their product. During the nineteen twenties, thirties and forties, Norman Rockwell, the great American artist, painted superb covers for the Saturday Evening Post and other periodicals in America, which depicted Santa Claus as a larger than life, loveable, grandfather figure.

The history of Father Christmas – Santa Claus, is long and complex. Many strands, through many centuries, and from different parts of the world have been intermingled and woven together to form the figure we are all familiar with today. As well as Saint Nicholas, there are elements of Saturn, Odin, Shamans and Nordic gnomes in his character. In recent times he has become a commercial icon far removed from the saintly Nicholas. He has evolved into a confusing mixture of Christian and pagan, fact and myth.

How does Father Christmas's descent down our chimneys come about and why should he ride in a sleigh drawn by flying reindeer? One school of thought says that this is American Indian in origin, whilst others defer to the theory that Laplanders, with their short red tunics and pointed hoods are responsible. Both peoples had shamans or witch-doctors and lucky spirits who were said to descend through the smoke-holes of their tepees or huts. During the long hard days of midwinter, drugs particularly fly agaric, were eaten to produce hallucinogenic trances which in turn induced a happy sense of well being and also a feeling of floating through the sky. The fen-people of Norfolk had a similar habit of drinking a brew of opium poppy heads soaked in brandy to ease their rheumatic joints and shut out the bitter cold, dampness and the darkness of winter. Reindeer are said to have a partiality for the fly agaric plant and perhaps this accounts for the notion that they too "flew" like men after partaking of this plant. A few fatalities must have taken place during these happy sessions as the plant is very poisonous when taken in excess.

Did the shaman descending the smokehole of Nordic peoples' shelters originate the idea of a flying Father Christmas who came down the sooty chimneys of Victorian England to fill the awaiting stockings? Maybe we will never know for sure. It would be ironic to think that a drug was originally responsible for the now harmless custom still believed in by small, innocent children.

These visits by Father Christmas or Santa Claus are, however, relatively recent in origin. Until Victorian times children were not singled out for undue attention at the Christmas festivities, and when gifts were given they were usually of a modest nature. In no way did they resemble the piles of expensive gifts which they receive today. They were truly small enough to fit into a child's stocking.

Christmas, in times past, was very much an adult affair, with feasting, rowdy behaviour and religious observance all mixed up together. Children enjoyed it as part of the family, but it was not specifically designed to please them. Probably they enjoyed the more active jollifications as much, or even more than their privileged descendants of today. After present opening most modern families sit down to watch television. Children have always enjoyed playing lively games much more than being passively fed with entertainment. The winter feast must have been doubly precious in the cold, dark, poverty-stricken days of long ago. Today's children, however, still look eagerly forward to the Yuletide celebrations. They write their letters to Father Christmas requesting various gifts, and what a joy it is to see all the wonder and magic of Christmas, reflected on the younger childrens' faces.

I think Saint Nicholas would approve.

A Victorian print showing a pagan image of Old Father Christmas riding the Yule Goat (Joulupukki); in one arm he holds the infant New Year and a basket containing gifts of food and wine, and in the other hand he carries a steaming Wassail bowl. The figure owes more to Odin than to Saint Nicholas, being a relic of pre- Christian festivities.

6

THE CHRISTMAS TREE

Dark green pyramid of light,
Glowing in the Christmas night.
Forest magic lit with stars,
Scent of pine brought from afar.

Monica Evans

One of the joys of Christmas is the dazzling tree smelling of pine forests, alight with colour, covered in twinkling fairy lights and topped with a silvery star. When the lights of the room are dimmed it shines out in the darkness like a pyramid of fire.

Strange to say, it is one of our more recent Christmas customs, only becoming popular in Britain during the past one hundred and fifty years, although trees had been an essential part of the Yule (Jul) festivities in Northern Europe for many hundreds of years. Our Christmas Tree probably came to us from Germany, when German princesses married to British kings and princes during the eighteenth and nineteenth centuries, set them up in the royal residences during the Christmas festivities.

It is recorded that Queen Charlotte, wife of George III, put up decorated trees for the amusement of her children at Christmas time in some of the royal palaces including Windsor Castle. Queen Adelaide, wife of William IV, decorated trees at Christmas with golden oranges, nuts and presents. Her much loved young niece Victoria, who was later to become queen, attended one of her Christmas parties and was delighted by the sight of the glittering tree. After her visit she wrote in her diary, *"We came home at half-past twelve. I was very much amused"*.

This event took place many years before Victoria's marriage to the German Prince Albert. It has been stated that he introduced the German custom of putting up decorated trees at Christmas in Britain, but it is evident that Queen Victoria already knew about them from her German aunt, Queen Adelaide.

Trees did not become generally popular until the 1840s when Queen Victoria and Prince Albert put one up and decorated it for their children at Windsor Castle. It became the central feature of their Christmas decorations and the idea soon spread when pictures of the royal couple standing by their tree were published in papers and magazines. Albert loved to continue with the customs of his homeland during the festivities in his newly adopted country. He never forgot his native land and was often homesick during his early years in Britain. Queen Victoria loved to please him and in 1841 she wrote in her diary:

"Today I have two children of my own to give presents to, who, they know not why, are full of happy wonder at the German Christmas Tree with its radiant candles......it quite affected dear Albert who turned pale, and had tears in his eyes and pressed my hand very warmly."

In December 1848 The Illustrated London News published the following description of the royal Christmas tree together with the above engraving showing Queen Victoria and Prince Albert, together with five of their children, standing in front of a glittering tree.

"*The Christmas tree in the engraving is that which is annually prepared by her Majesty's command for the Royal children....The tree employed for this festive purpose is a young fir of about eight feet high, and has six tiers of branches. On each tier, or branch, are arranged a dozen wax tapers. Pendant from the branches are elegant trays, baskets, bonbonnieres, and other receptacles for sweetmeats of the most varied and expensive kind; and of all forms, colours and degrees of beauty. Fancy cakes, gilt gingerbread and eggs filled with sweetmeats, are also suspended by variously-coloured ribbons from the branches. The tree, which stands upon a table covered with white damask, is supported at the root by piles of sweets of a larger kind, and by toys and dolls of all descriptions, suited to the youthful fancy, and to the several ages of the interesting scions of Royalty for whose gratification they are displayed. The tree was constructed and arranged by Mr Mawdill, the Queen's confectioner."*

The custom of setting up and decorating a small pine tree during the Christmas celebrations soon spread across Victorian England. Households of the rich right down to the poor embraced the custom which was so new and at the same time so ancient. Strange to say, the original Christmas tree was said to have been devised by an Englishman, St.Boniface of Crediton, in Devon, who lived during the eighth century. He was an early missionary to the pagan Germanic tribes living in the dark Teutonic forests of that time.

The story goes that he found a group of Germans about to sacrifice a young boy to the sacred oak. He was horrified by the idea of blood sacrifice and hacked down the great oak and as it fell to the ground a small fir tree, which had been growing amongst its great roots, was revealed.

"Take this", he said, pointing to the little tree, *"as a symbol of new life and hope".* A candle was placed by it to symbolise the Light of the World coming down to us at Christmastide. The custom soon spread across Germany with the coming of Christianity and later on to the rest of Europe.

Martin Luther was reputed to have decorated a tree with candles and fruits for his children in the sixteenth century. He is said to have thought of the idea after staring up into the starry sky on a clear frosty winter's night. The twinkling stars above his head put into his mind the idea of a small tree covered with tiny, lighted candles, shining out into the darkness of his home at Christmas time.

It is almost certain that lights on trees existed long before this date, however, as Nordic peoples believed in Yggdrasil, the great world tree which represented all things living in nature and linked heaven, earth and the Norse hell. The fate of the world depended upon this tree and its branches spread over the universe; of its many roots, one reached to Aesir, another to the giants, a third one went to Niflheim, where was Hvergelmir, the fountain from which all the waters of the earth originated. Under another root was Nidhogg a dragon who perpetually gnawed its roots. Mimur's well was under its second root and Urdhr's fountain was under its first. It was at this place that the Norse gods met daily to give judgement. Odin sacrificed himself on this tree, piercing himself through with a spear and hanging thus for nine days whilst he acquired wisdom with which to rule heaven and earth.

It is interesting to note that the Cross upon which Christ was crucified is frequently referred to as "The Tree", especially in medieval writings. Could this be a survival of the ancient Norse beliefs?

Norsemen too celebrated Yule, or Jul, which was their equivalent of the Christian Christmas, with lights in their dwellings and branches of evergreens brought inside as decorations and tributes to their gods. Our present day Christmas tree seems to have glowed down through the centuries from very primitive times. The sparkling star which twinkles from the topmost spike of the Yuletide spruce represents the Star of Bethlehem, shining out to announce Christ's birth and to guide the Three Wise Men to the scene of the Nativity. Probably this star was the symbol used to Christianise a pagan object. Tree worship was an integral part of many primitive religions, for trees were considered to be the source of life with power being channeled into their great roots by the gods of nature, by which mankind survived and continued the race. Until comparatively recent times woodmen would ask forgiveness of a tree before felling commenced. Trees such as oak, elder, holly, rowan and willow were considered to be so sacred that men avoided cutting them down or destroying them; likewise to have such a tree on your land brought good luck and protection from misfortune.

Our recent ecological studies bear out this belief that trees are indeed an essential part of life on earth giving us protection and providing purifying elements to our atmosphere. Maybe our more primitive ancestors were not so gullible as they would at first appear to be.

There is a legend which says that at the hour on which Christ is said to have been born all the trees in the forest burst into leaf and bloom in spite of the frosts and snows of midwinter.

The Glastonbury thorn *(Crataegus monogyna biflora),* which is said to have originally sprung and taken root from Joseph of Arimathea's staff whilst he rested at Glastonbury, still blooms with delicate, whitish-pink blossoms every Christmastide. Sprays of this blossom are sent annually to the reigning sovereign for use in their floral decorations during the Christmas festival. This tree too would seem to symbolize the springtime which lies just a few months ahead bringing with it fertility and hopefully plenteous crops.

The people of Norway send a giant Norwegian Spruce fir tree to England every December. It is erected in Trafalgar Square right in the heart of London. It's hundreds of twinkling lights send a message of goodwill to onlookers. It is an annual "thank you" gift for the support and sacrifices made by British forces in World War II during their fight for the liberation of Norway from their Nazi invaders.

It is customary not to decorate a Christmas tree until Christmas Eve. In Victorian times it was done secretly by the adults with glittering baubles, little gifts (by those who could afford them) and tiny candles, then late on Christmas Eve the room was darkened, its doors flung open to reveal the Christmas tree in all its shimmering glory to the excited children of the house. What an impact that must have made, especially in the days before the media was able to surfeit our eyes and ears with the sights and sounds of Christmas from October onwards.

The tree should always have its decorations taken down on Twelfth Night. It is thought to be unlucky to leave them up beyond that date. The bare tree must never be carelessly discarded on a rubbish tip but burnt in the sacred element of fire. What you do with an old tree in a centrally heated flat is open to question! Maybe this is why the plastic trees have become so popular, though I don't think the spirit of any god dwelt in these soul-less objects.

The joy of a fresh, sweet scented pine cannot be imitated even if it does shed its needles all over the floor. May we all enjoy the beauty of our Yuletide trees for many generations to come.

A Child's Song

Christmas tree, oh, Christmas tree,
Shining here for you and me.
Christmas tree, oh, Christmas tree,
The prettiest sight you'll ever see :
Christmas tree, oh Christmas tree,
Green, scented branches of delight,
Bringing joy on a Christmas night.

Monica Evans

7

CANDLES, LAMPS and LANTERNS

Torches, torches, run with torches,
All the way to Bethlehem!
Christ is born and now he's sleeping;
Come and sing your song to him.

An old Galician Carol

"Let those who have no light in themselves light candles!... Let those over whom hell fire is hanging fix to their doors laurels doomed presently to burn! You are the light of the world, you are the tree ever green".

Tertullian. 160-230 A.D.

Tertullian, or Quintus Septimus Florens Tertullianus was one of the earliest Latin ecclesiastical writers.

The sight of a friendly golden light shining out from a window into the darkness of a winter's night has always been a welcome sight to man. This was especially so in the days before street lighting arrived upon the scene, or electricity shone from every house even in the depths of the countryside. It is hard for us to imagine how black a night could be to our ancestors. Light, therefore, has always formed a special role in the festivities and rites of mankind right across the world.

"Sir Henry de Barton, native of Mildenhall, Suffolk, Master of the Skinners' Company, Lord Mayor of London, decreed in 1416 that lanterns with lights be lighted on evenings between Hallontide (Hallowstide) and Candlemas."

An inscription from Melton Mowbray Parish Church showing a bequest for lights between November 1st (All Hallows), and February 2nd (Candlemas).

Before the days of candles, small pottery and bronze oil lamps were used similar to the ones we see in illustrations dealing with Roman life. The very poorest people resorted to rush-lights or tallow dips. These were simply twisted dried rushes soaked in animal fat, to form a taper which was then fixed with a metal grip and afterwards set alight. These dips smelt vile, smoked, and gave a very dim light, but it was better than no illumination at all. Candles remained expensive luxuries for the rich until comparatively recent times. Most religions in the world have festivals of light even in the far away countries such as Japan and India. The use of lamps and torches formed an important part of the cult of Mithras in ancient Persia and Rome.

Hanukkah, the Jewish Festival of Lights, falls at roughly the same time as our Christmas, and it is easy to forget that many of the Jewish festivals and services formed the basis of our Christian rites. Christ would have been familiar with the Festival of Light, and he told the parable of the unwise virgins who allowed their lamps to burn dry at a wedding celebration.

Candles and lamps, therefore, go back into the mists of time long before history could be recorded. Customs, however, die-hard, and are passed down from one generation to another, often when the original celebration has been forgotten, or changed by succeeding people beyond all recognition. To primitive and pagan man fire and light represented the sun, welcome warmth and fertility, but to Christians it represented the coming of the new sun in the person of Christ.

An early Syrian Christian wrote: *"The reason why the Fathers transferred the celebration of Christ's birth from the sixth of January to the twentyfifth of December was this: It is the custom of the heathen to celebrate on the same twentyfifth of December as the birthday of the sun, at which they kindled lights in token of festivity. In these solemnities and festivities the Christians also took part. Accordingly when the doctors of the church perceived that the Christians had a leaning to this festival, they took counsel and resolved that the true Nativity should be solemnised on that day and the festival of the Epiphany on the sixth of January. Accordingly, along with this custom, the practice has prevailed of kindling fires till the sixth."*

It can be seen that this is the origin of our Twelve Days of Christmas between Christmas Day and the Feast of the Epiphany.

When Saint Augustine converted many of the English to Christianity in the sixth century, he too warned the new converts, *"not to celebrate the solemn birthday of the Son of God like the heathen on account of the sun, but because of Him who made the sun and all mankind"*.

The Celtic tribes had been accustomed to a festival of fire and light in honour of Brigit, their fire goddess, at around this date in midwinter.

Many churches today have an Advent Candle which is lit on the first Sunday of Advent, roughly four weeks before Christmas. The candle is marked off into four sections and the subsequent three parts are lit on the following Sundays before the Feast of Nativity.

Candles were in the past (and indeed still are) very expensive items, especially the large ones used in churches, synagogues etc. as they are made from the finest beeswax. They are only lit on special occasions and symbolise the enlightenment of mankind.

Mr R.T.Hampson wrote down the following observations in 1841:
"In some places candles are made of a particular kind, because the candle that is lighted on Christmas Day must be so large as to burn from the time of its ignition to the close of the day, otherwise it will portend evil to the family for the ensuing year. The poor were wont to present the rich with wax tapers, and Yule candles are still in the north of Scotland given by merchants to their customers. At one time children at the village schools in Lancashire were required to bring each a mould candle before the parting, or separation for the Christmas holidays."

How beautiful it is to hear the old carols ringing out in a church lit entirely by candles. The atmosphere seems to take us back to bygone days long ago when our forebears worshipped in much the same way. The famous candlelit service of Nine Lessons and Carols from Kings' College, Cambridge, is now seen and heard on television and radio all over the world, and has become a very important part of Christmas Eve to many people.

Not all our candlelit celebrations are so impressive. Most people have a candle or two on their dinner tables at Christmastide, and some have them burning in decorated candlesticks or flower arrangements over the festive period much as their pagan ancestors did. The little candles on Christmas trees are said to represent the star of Bethlehem which heralded Christ's birth.

In Scandinavia a candle has always been the symbol of hospitality, friendship and hope. Their Norse ancestors valued the luxury of light during their extremely long winter nights. Candles are lit by Danes, Norwegians and Swedes whenever a guest is entertained no matter what the time of year, and very welcoming they look.

The festival of Saint Lucia (Lucy) on December thirteenth is celebrated by the Scandinavians and marks the beginning of the Jul

(Yule) festivities. On this day in Sweden and Denmark, a young girl, or virgin as they put it more bluntly in the past, is chosen to represent Saint Lucia who lived from 281-304 A.D in Syracuse, Italy. She was betrothed to a wealthy pagan man against her will and refused to give up her Christian faith and marry him. This so enraged her suitor that he denounced her as a Christian to the Roman Governor Paschasius who sentenced her to have her eyes put out and to be beheaded. She is one of the virgin martyrs who became popular during the Middle Ages, and because of her barbarous torture was made patron saint of the blind.

Often the eldest unmarried daughter in a Swedish family is chosen to be St.Lucia, and on the saint's feast day she gets up early and dresses herself in a white gown representing purity with a red sash symbolising the martyr's blood. On her head she wears a crown of evergreens into which are placed lighted candles. With this glowing crown alight she then serves her family with coffee and little cakes or saffron buns. This ceremony is much looked forward to by the young Swedish girls. Often towns appoint a municipal Saint Lucia and the lucky girl parades through the streets accompanied by other young people carrying burning torches. The idea of the flaming crown probably pre-dates the Saint Lucia festival by hundreds of years and originally symbolised Brigit, or Bride, the pagan goddess of fire and fertility.

In Ireland it used to be the custom, and probably still is in some areas, for twelve candles to be lit at Christmas plus a larger one to represent Christ and his disciples. Ordinary families lit a special Christmas candle which was often placed in a window. If possible it was lighted by a girl named Mary or, failing that, by the youngest girl present on Christmas Day. It was extinguished, after burning all day, by the oldest man in the household.

In Britain we still see carol singers singing their way around the villages and towns during the weeks prior to Christmas, and many of them have lanterns in which burns a candle, in spite of the fact that electric torches exist and street lighting shines out in the darkness. It may be an anachronism but we all welcome the sight of these bobbing, flickering lanterns illuminating the faces of the carollers, or waits, on a cold winter night.

Candlemas on February 2nd is the Feast of the Purification of the Blessed Virgin Mary, and it also celebrates the Presentation of the Infant Christ in the Temple. During the Middle Ages the religious celebration of Christmas went beyond the Twelve Days, and Candlemas marked the close of the Christmas celebrations. During the Mass the church would be lit by many pure white candles, and placed around the church would be bowls of snowdrops: Candlemas Bells, Mary's Tapers, Fair Maids of February are some of the old names used for this delicate winter flower. It must have been an enchanting sight to see the tiny white flowers and the glowing candles all around during the service. It is said that snowdrops were especially planted in monastery gardens and churchyards for this reason and maybe that is why we find them still growing in great clumps in these places. All the candles which were to be used during the church year were dedicated and blessed during this service. The lights of midwinter festivities have twinkled down to us from the feast of Saturn, Mithras in Persia, Brigit the Celtic fire goddess, and the Star of Bethlehem.

They are still glowing brightly as an integral part of our celebrations today.

> *The holly's up, the house is all bright,*
> *The tree is ready, the candles alight:*
> *Rejoice and be glad all children tonight.*
>
> German "Christbaum" Carol
> Peter Cornelius

8

THE YULE LOG

"See the blazing Yule before us,
Fa la la la la la la la la,
Strike the harp and join the chorus,
Fa la la la la la la la la."
Traditional Welsh Carol

It is rare to find a really large Yule log burning during the Christmas festivities today. Our modern hearths scarcely accommodate a small log and many houses rely entirely on gas or electric heating.

The great Yule log once played a very important part in our winter celebrations. Often it was enormous, half a tree or part of a great oak or ash, for it had to last over the twelve days of Christmas, slowly burning away. Only the huge fireplaces in the great halls of castles and mansions could accommodate them. Poorer people made do with smaller versions, often faggots which were bundles of twigs bound tightly together and several of these bundles would be, in turn, trussed together to form a substantial piece of kindling. Peasants in medieval Britain were often given rights to gather such fuel for their homes, and the enclosures during the eighteenth century brought much suffering in this respect when these ancient rights were denied to them.

Like most of our customs the history of the Yule log goes back to our pagan past as tree worship has formed part of many ancient religions. The life force of nature was believed to be channelled into the trees by the gods. Woodsmen often said a prayer to a tree and begged its forgiveness before cutting it down, for it was a task not lightly undertaken, and to cut down such trees as elder, holly and willow was absolutely taboo. Would that our modern contractors were so careful!

In Viking times great oak logs were burnt during the winter festival of Jul, in honour of the god Thor who was the deity connected with the oak tree and, incidentally, thunder. It was probably this connection which caused pieces of the charred Yule log to be kept as charms to ward off thunder and lightning. In the days of timber houses, fire could destroy a family and its wealth very quickly. Precious hay and straw was lost if struck by lightning. The Celts held fire to be so sacred that a perpetual fire was kept burning in the great halls with a fire keeper in charge to see that it was always kept alight. We can see how important this was in the days before matches and lighters were invented. Creating fire was an arduous and tedious procedure.

The great fire festivals of pagan Europe fell during the summer solstice (Midsummer) and the winter solstice (Midwinter or Jul). On Midsummer night great outdoor bonfires were lit, and indeed still are in the Scandinavian countries, but during the winter the fires were lighted inside buildings as well, to promote warmth and cheer during the coldest time of the year. These winter fires symbolised the return of the sun to the earth in springtime, bringing with it fertility to the land and also the purifying qualities of fire. Fire drove away the demons and harmful influences in a building and it also purified by sterilising any contaminated objects, as indeed it does to this day.

Before antiseptics and sterilising equipment were invented the heat of a fire was mankind's only reliable purifier and of course it was one of the four sacred elements.

In the past it was thought that a house would be protected from witchcraft for as long as the Yule log burned. The remains of the charred log were carefully preserved both to protect the household from fire and lightning and also to ignite the new Yule log during the Christmas festivities of the following year.

> *They pile the Yule-log on the hearth*
> *Soak toasted crabs in ale;*
> *And while they sip, them homely rivith*
> *Is joyous as if all the earth*
> *For man were void of bale.*

Baron's Yule Feast – A Christmas Rhyme
Thomas Cooper 1846

In Germany, during days gone by, a great oak tree trunk was firmly fixed into a hearth as part of its foundation. A fire was lighted on top of this and the oak underneath burnt away only very slowly lasting a whole year when it was replaced by a new log on the following Christmas Eve. The old charred log was used to re-kindle the new fire.

A seventeenth century French writer was sceptical about the belief that a burnt remnant of log would provide insurance against fire and other mishaps. He wrote:

"It is believed that a log called a trefoir or Christmas brand, which you put on the fire on Christmas Eve and continue to burn for a little while every day until Twelfth Night can, if kept under the bed, protect the house for a whole year from fire and thunder....that it can prevent inmates from having chilblains on their heels in winter and cure cattle of many maladies and wheat from mildew."

Like most of our ancient pagan customs the Church sought to

Christianise them since they were unable to totally subdue them. One of the woods which was used for Yule logs was the ash and there is an old legend which explains why this is so.

It is said that when Christ was born in the stable at Bethlehem, Joseph could not find any dry wood with which to kindle a fire to warm Mary and the Child. He saw an ash tree growing nearby and cut some branches off to light a fire so that the Infant Christ could be bathed and warmed by its heat. Since that time the ash is one of the few woods which burn well in a green state.

> *"Ashwood green and Ashwood brown*
> *Is fit for a queen in a golden crown,*
> *Ashwood wet and Ashwood dry*
> *A king may warm his slippers by"*
>
> Traditional

Another version of this story says the shepherds visiting the manger made a fire of ashwood for the comfort of Mary and baby Jesus.

Yule logs or Christbrands, as they were often known, were brought in from the woods to the great houses with great ceremony and jollification. They were hauled along by a group of strong men with ropes, whilst other people sang carols and waved branches of evergreens to accompany its transportation.

The Yule Log

> *Come, bring with noise,*
> *My merrie, merrie boyes,*
> *The Christmas Log to the firing;*
> *While my good Dame, she*
> *Bids ye all be free;*
> *And drink to your hearts desiring.*

With the last yeeres brand
Light the new block, and
For good success in his spending,
On your Psalteries play,
That sweet luck may
Come while the log is a tending.

Robert Herrick..(1591-1674)

(Robert Herrick, a friend of "rare Ben Jonson", was Vicar of Dean Prior near Totnes in Devon. He must have seen many country Christmases and wrote several poems which featured the customs of his day.)

On reaching the great hall the log was manoeuvred into position on the enormous open fireplace and lit on Christmas Eve by the charred remnant of the former year's log. This gigantic log was supported on fire-dogs and fed into the fire a little at a time and so it continued to burn slowly right through the twelve days of the Christmas feast. John Brand, an eighteenth century antiquary wrote the following words in his "Observations on Popular Antiquities":

"Our ancestors were wont to light up candles of uncommon size, called Christmas candles, and lay a log of wood upon the fire called a Yule-log or Christmas-block to illuminate the house, and, as it were, to turn night into day."

In these days of instant lighting it is easy to forget how much a good blazing fire contributed to the illumination of a room. Candles alone made a cheerless atmosphere and many poor people could not afford even this modest form of lighting and sat in the firelight on a winter's evening. As well as promising heat and light the kitchen fire was the only form of cooking facility available to ordinary folk in early times. It must be admitted that there is something comforting in the flames of a fire flickering out into a darkened room.

Ashes from the Yule log used to be scattered on the ploughed fields in order to fertilise them and promote good growth during the coming year: it is, without doubt, a good source of potash for the soil.

Instead of having a Christmas cake, the French have a Buche de Noël or chocolate log, which is decorated to resemble a real log, and finally dusted with icing sugar to simulate frost or snow. They have become popular in England during recent years and they are as near as most people get to having a Yule log in their homes in these modern times of central heating; it is, however, a sad substitute for the blazing fires of old.

It may be seen that fires not only gave warmth and light but they were also the only source of hot, wholesome food. Keeping a fire continuously burning was of paramount importance to our ancestors, and fire came to symbolise comfort, plenty and light, being to them, a blessing from the gods.

The Yule log has survived the centuries often in name only but it remains a powerful symbol, representing warmth, joy and hospitality long after its pagan associations have been forgotten by most people.

> "The block behind the fire is put
> To sanction customs old desires
> And many a faggots bands are cut
> For the old farmers Christmass fires
> Where loud tong'd gladness joins the throng
> And winter meets the warmth of May.
> Feeling by times the heat too strong
> And rubs his shins and draws away".
>
> John Clare   1827

9

CHRISTMAS CARDS

Now stand bright cards all in a row along the chimney breast,
Sent by those who, in this life, we cherish and love the best.
Bright designs showing Christmas scenes and robins in the snow,
All set out gaily side by side amongst the holly and mistletoe.

Monica Evans

The sending of cards to our friends and relatives at Christmas time is a relatively modern custom, dating from late Victorian times. The first painted cards appeared during the 1840s and there are several contenders for the honour of inventing Christmas cards. The first was Sir Henry Cole, founder of the Victoria and Albert Museum. He asked John Calcott Horsley to make a design for him.

A hand-coloured lithograph design was produced in 1843 (?) and a thousand prints were made and sold at Felix Summerley's Treasure House in Bond Street. The venture was not a commercial success, which is not surprising as they cost one shilling each which must have been very expensive in those days.

The second contender was a card designed for William Maw Egley in either 1843 or 1848. As the printing of the numerals is not clear it could be either of these two dates. If the first date is correct then this is the earlier of the two designs.

W.C.T.Dobson, R.A., designed a card which was appropriate to the season and sent it to a friend in 1844. It was a success and the next year he had copies printed and sent them to a wider circle of friends.

The Reverend Edward Bradley, a writer living in Newcastle during the 1840s, had a card made for himself so that he could send them to his friends at Christmastide.

Perhaps we will never know which card was the very first one sent as there may have been others which have not survived the years. The Victoria and Albert Museum have original copies of the John Horsley and William Maw Egley cards. Early Victorian cards are extremely rare and they are eagerly snapped up by collectors. It is interesting to note that the goodwill message on these cards remains the same on many of our modern designs: *"A Merry Christmas and a Happy New Year"*.

The above design (1843) is reputed to be one
of the first – ever Christmas cards.
(Victoria & Albert museum)

Before the advent of Christmas cards, letters of greeting and family remembrance were written to relatives and friends. This, of course, was a habit only indulged in by the rich and leisured classes, as few working class people could read or write in those days.

Three things contributed to the popularisation of the Christmas card. Firstly, the invention of cheap and efficient colour printing in 1860 enabled cards to be reproduced at reasonable prices. Secondly, the Elementary Education Act of 1870 meant that even the poor and working classes learnt to read and write. It is of little use either sending or receiving a card if you can't address it or tell from whom it came. Thirdly, a halfpenny postage rate was introduced in 1870 for cards or notes sent in unsealed envelopes. The normal rate was a penny for ordinary letters.

Cards quickly became popular and, by 1880, the Postmaster General was pleading for people to "Post early for Christmas!" People were even beginning to complain about the delay caused to ordinary correspondence by the excessive amount of Christmas mail, in spite of the fact that there were five deliveries a day in large cities.

Special Christmas stationery was first advertised in the December edition of The Illustrated London News in 1863. The earliest massed produced cards were printed in sheets and resembled coloured postcards which could be torn off by the customer as required. Postcard type greeting cards were popular right up to the 1940s. Many of the early cards were not at all Christmassy, having designs of flowers surrounded by lacey cut paper work. They resembled Valentine cards more than our familiar Christmas cards, for the Victorian printers used the plates of Valentine cards and merely added an appropriate Christmas greeting. Seasonal designs soon outnumbered these fancy designs as cards became more and more popular.

Raphael Tuck & Sons, the printers, were quick to see the commercial possibilities of greeting cards and the firm became famous for well-printed colourful designs based on many differing themes.

The much coveted Royal Appointment award and insignia was granted to them in 1893. Cards had come a long way in only a little over forty years.

Comical cards were produced, and even to our modern eyes many appear very cruel to the recipient. The Victorians and Edwardians were not so prim as many people imagine them to be.

Shops used to send out cards and calendars to regular and valued customers at Christmas time and in the New Year. There are records of shopkeepers complaining of the cost, and how, if they didn't send them, they lost the goodwill of their customers who transferred their custom to more generous establishments. The blandishments idea of free gifts is not a new one!

During the first World War cards embroidered in silk were sent home by the men serving in France. Many of these survive having been kept carefully stored away by the wives and sweethearts of soldiers who were never to return to these shores. Often these cards showed patriotic symbols such as the flags of allied nations as well as little scenes and flowery designs. Sometimes they held a seasonal greeting and often a patriotic one.

A 1914-18 embroidered greetings card

Christmas cards from all periods are collected by keen enthusiasts. Queen Mary, our Queen's grandmother, was one of the first people to begin building up a large collection of greetings cards. It is a good idea to paste favourite cards or ones from special friends and relatives in a scrap book. Much joy can be had from looking over cards received in years gone by. It is also interesting to note the change in design through the various eras. However, the message remains the same whatever the outward design.

A Silk embroidered Christmas card
sent from France during WWI (1914-18)

10

ROBINS

*Little Robin-Redbreast
To the window comes,
Seeking warmth and shelter
Asking us for crumbs.
Shall we not remember
All outside our door,
Whom the chill December
Finds hungry, sad and poor?*

A rhyme from a Victorian
Christmas card signed M.J.J.

Exactly why we use robins so much on our Christmas cards, wrapping paper and gift tags is a matter for conjecture. There are various theories as to why this is so and certainly this little bird has several legends woven around him which have interesting links with both pagan and Christian religions.

He is our national bird, although this title was only recently bestowed upon him. Unlike many birds familiar to us in town and countryside he remains in Britain throughout the year braving the cold of winter. The other native birds which remain with us during the winter months do not sing at this time but Robin's voice can be heard with its sweet high trills on even the coldest day. Robins are said to choose their mates in December which seems a cold time for courting! In medieval times it was thought to be one of the creatures who were the familiars of witches. This is probably because they are so fearless and unafraid of man. They are always on the look-out for an easy meal and their shining black eyes never miss a worm turned up by the gardener or a crumb thrown out by a housewife. Often they will come up to a window and tap with their beaks for food. No doubt this was thought to be devilish and unbirdlike behaviour during the Middle Ages.

There are several legends connected with the robin.

One is of pagan origin and tells how all the birds quarrelled as they could not decide which of their number should have the title King of All the Birds. It was decided that the bird who flew the highest should claim the title. All of them took flight and flew up and ever upwards. Gradually most of them dropped out of the contest until only the eagle was left. Now, unbeknown to him, a tiny wren had secreted itself amongst the feathers on his back. Eventually even the eagle tired of the long climb and dropped earthwards, but the wren continued to climb until it got so close to the sun that it caught fire. Down, down the little bird plunged towards the earth with flaming feathers. His friend the robin saw his plight and threw himself upon the wren attempting to put out the flames, but the wren died and the robin's breast was scorched red by the searing flames. The wren was declared King of the Birds because of his daring but it was the robin who brought fire to mankind and why he still has a redbreast.

There are two other stories which have a Christian slant to them. The first one goes as follows:

When Christ was hanging on the Cross at Golgotha a robin flew past and saw the poor suffering man with blood pouring down his face caused by the cruel crown of thorns pressed into his brow. Now at this time robin was a rather dull looking bird, all brown and grey. When he saw Christ's plight he flew up to Him hanging there on the Cross, and attempted to pull out the thorns which were piercing His brow. In doing so, robin's breast became stained with the blood of Christ and it has remained that way from that day to this as a sign of his compassion.

Another story tells how robin flew down to hell for he was curious to see how men fared there. When he heard the screams of the sinners damned for eternity to dwell in the searing heat of hell, he was so distressed and unhappy that he flew back up to earth and collected a small leather pouch full of water so that the souls in torment might drink and quench their thirst. The flames of hell were too much for the little bird and they beat him back, and the water dried up. As he struggled to escape from the fire his breast was scorched by the flames and instead of a dull brown chest it was turned to the rusty red we all see today. It has remained that way ever since and he was known henceforth as Robin-Redbreast in honour of his brave deeds.

In all these legends it is the robin's friendliness and compassion which is the main point of the story. Men throughout the ages must have taken pleasure from his proximity and companionship. He has always been connected with stories of fire for obvious reasons and it is understandable that during the fire festivals of the winter solstice this little bird should be the one chosen to represent the comfort and warmth which fire brings to man in the cold days of winter. What a joy it is to see his bright orangey red-breast shining out amongst the snow and frost during the bitter days of wintertime. He is, of course, a fierce fighter towards other birds of his kind and defends his territory with great courage and ferocity at times. No doubt his red breast is really a warning-off signal, a danger, beware sign. To most of us, however, he is a delightful creature who epitomises the cheerfulness of Christmastide festivities.

Another theory offered as to why the robin is so popular with us at Christmas time is the fact that the postmen in early Victorian times wore long, bright red jackets or frock-coats, together with dark blue trousers and a top hat. They were nick-named "Robin Redbreasts" because of these scarlet coats. Their visits to each house were eagerly awaited especially at Christmas time, for mail being delivered to each door was a new innovation in those days. We take it for granted now, but it is understandable how popular these red-coated postmen became during the early years of Victoria's reign.

Robin Redbreast

Welcome, little Robin,
With your scarlet breast,
In this winter weather
Cold must be your nest.
Hopping on the hard ground,
Picking up the crumbs,
Robin knows the children
Love him when he comes.

Anon

"Nowell sing we ...."

This illustration is based on a medieval roof boss in Beverley Minster

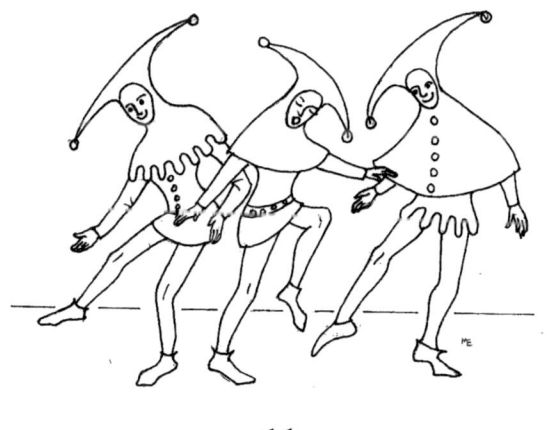

11

CAROLS and MUMMERS

Come down tomorrow night and mind
Don't leave the fiddle bag behind
We'll shake a leg and drink a cup
Of ale and keep old Christmas up.
And every one shall tell his tale,
And every one shall sing his song,
And every one will drink his ale
To love and friendship all night long.

Christmas Invitation. William Barnes

Christmas would not be the same without the lovely carols from the past and the present day which give such a beautiful and atmospheric background to our Christmas celebrations.

The word carol is derived from the medieval French CAROLE, which meant a dance performed in a large circle often accompanied by a lively chorus. Some authorities believe that the two Latin words

CANTARE (to sing) and ROLA (joyous) formed the basis of this French word CAROLE.

These ring-dances were performed throughout the Middle Ages, across Europe during the great church festivals such as Easter, Christmas, etc., and indeed they also had a place in the more secular May Day festivities. Churches, in those days, were without pews, and only the aged and sick people had a bench provided for them which was set against the church wall, hence the saying, "the weakest go to the wall". Rich and influential personages were provided with carved seats, and monks were able to recline against misericords in the choir-stalls, however, ordinary folk stood throughout the long services. During the main religious festivals, and especially at Easter and Christmas, the congregation would make large circles and dance around the pillars of the churches which were unencumbered by pews and formed an ideal area for communal dances. Many early medieval carols have lovely, lilting melodies which still set our feet tapping and it can easily be understood how they were especially written with dancing in mind. God was praised joyously in song and dance on these occasions. In the fourteenth century Geoffrey Chaucer wrote :-

> "Come, and if it lyke you
> To dauncen, dauncith with us now.
> And I, without tarrying
> Went into the karolying."

In Brittany these ring-dances are still performed during certain festivals, though now they more often take place in the streets than in a church. Often ale was consumed at the back of the church after such celebratory services and, in consequence, things became rather rowdy and unmanageable; so much so that the church eventually banned dancing and drinking in church, leaving only the joyous music which was sung, usually in Latin, by the choir and sometimes the congregation. Carol, then, came to mean a festive song for a specific church festival, not only Christmas, but also Advent, Epiphany, Easter, Whitsun, and even May Day and Harvest.

Many of the European medieval carols have beautiful words which often allude to the customs and way of life at that period of time. The Virgin Mary was frequently depicted as a *"Lady of high degree", "a lily fair", "a rose", "heavenly Queen"*. People in the Middle Ages could not envisage the figure of Mary as a lowly Jewess in the colonial Roman province of Judah. The Virgin became an idolised and romantic figure far removed from the everyday figure of ordinary motherhood. Modern carols have put a new and probably more factual slant on the words of present day compositions.

During the thirteenth century, St.Francis of Assisi and his companions seem to have been amongst the first people to popularise the more sacred and solemn type of hymn which celebrated Christ's birth.

Jacopone of Todi, one of Saint Francis of Assisi's followers, was reputed to have been the first person to produce Christian songs and carols in the common tongue of the people instead of Latin. He was a strange man much given to self-mortification, and he was so eccentric in his habits that even the early Franciscans found him difficult to cope with. He did, however, produce beautiful and joyous sacred songs and carols. John Addington Symonds, in his book "The Renaissance in Italy" writes, Jacopone was *"the man who struck the key-note in religious popular poetry"*.

An extract from a translation by Symonds of Jacopone's Il Presèpio (The Manger) goes as follows:

Come and look upon her child
Nestling in the hay!
See his fair arms opened wide,
On her lap to play!
And she tucks him by her side,
Cloaks him as she may:
Gives her paps unto his mouth,
Where his lips are laid.

For the little babe had drouth,
Sucked the breast she gave;
All he sought was that sweet breast,
Broth he did not crave;
With his tiny mouth he pressed
Tiny mouth that clave:
Ah, the tiny baby thing,
Mouth to bosom laid!

Little angels all around
Danced, and carols flung;
Making verselets sweet and true,
Still of love they sung;
Calling saints and sinners too
With love's tender tongue;
Now that heaven's high glory is
On this earth displayed...

Jacopone died on Christmas Day 1306, an apt day for the author of so many lovely Christmas songs and religious poems.

Not all carols were sung in church during former centuries. Waits used to travel around towns and the countryside playing upon simple musical instruments and singing local carols. Originally waits were night-watchmen, the predecessors of our policemen, who carried musical instruments perhaps to while away the long night-time duties. This night-watch or town-watch, not only patrolled the streets keeping a look out for criminals during the hours of darkness, but they also called out the hours, a necessary service in bygone days when few people possessed watches or clocks.

This custom is celebrated in the following lines from an old carol:

Past two o'clock, and a cold frosty morning.
Past two o'clock, good morrow, masters all.

Often they were employed at Christmas time and sometimes other festivals, by the town authorities to play in the local square and streets. Later their duties as watchmen lapsed and they were purely local musicians employed by the municipality on special occasions. One of the earliest records of town waits comes from Exeter and is dated 1400.

In medieval York, mistletoe was set upon the high altar and a pardon was proclaimed for miscreants. Heralds blew a fanfare of trumpets from York's four barrs (gates) and everyone, no matter how poor, was welcomed to the city. The people gathered at the gates and cried, "Ule, Ule, Ule! It is good to cry Ule!" Waits performed their music and sang their Christmas songs throughout the city.

It was customary for householders and farmers to refresh the waits with a piece of mincepie or cake and some liquid refreshment, which must have been most welcome to the group after an often long, cold trek through the streets or countryside. Sometimes the Wassail Bowl was presented full of steaming hot spiced ale or wine. A few such convivial visits must have made for unsteady footsteps on the homeward journey, and no doubt the words of the carols became more and more indistinct as the night progressed!

> Here we come a-wassailing among the leaves so green,
> Here we come a-wandering, so fair to be seen.
> *Chorus:*
> *Love and joy come to you, and to you your wassail too,*
> *And God bless you, and send you a happy New Year.*
> *And God send you a happy New Year.*

Waits and their accompanying musicians were not always welcome. One irate householder writing in the eighteenth century reported that:

"The waits are detached bodies of impromptu musicians, who make the night hideous for three weeks before Christmas with their wretched performances of indifferent melodies"

Even at sea the tradition of singing carols and playing music on Christmas Day was maintained.

In 1675 the following entry was recorded by a Mr Teonge in his diary whilst on board an English man-of-war.

> "Christmas day wee keep thus: At 4 in the morning our trumpeters all doe flat their trumpets, and begin at our Captain's cabin, and thence to all the officers, and gentleman's cabins, playing a levite at each cabine door, and bidding good morrow, wishing a merry Crismas. After they goe to their station, viz. on the _ope (poop), and sound 3 levitts in honour of the morning. At 10 wee goe to prayers and sermon, text Zacc. ix,, 9".

It has become a tradition for the Salvation Army Bands to play in towns and cities during the busy shopping days prior to Christmas. These bands are the nearest thing we have to the old waits, and the sound of the old familiar carols sounding out into the cold winter air continues to give many people a little thrill of pleasure.

Children have, for centuries, gone around singing carols from door to door, and receiving alms in return. This additional money provided a few rare treats, and a little extra food for the Christmas festivities, amongst the poor during past centuries.

> We are not daily beggars, that beg from door to door,
> But we are neighbours' children whom you have seen before.
> Chorus:
>   Love and joy come to you ...... etc..
>
> We have got a little purse of stretching leather skin;
> We want a little money to line it well within.
> Chorus:
>   Love and joy come to you ...... etc..
>
> God bless the master of this house, like wise the mistress too;
> And all the little children that round the table go.
> Chorus:
>   Love and joy come to you ...... etc..

In recent years, fewer and fewer young voices are heard outside our doors during the run up to Christmas: maybe television distracts them, perhaps the streets are no longer a safe place in which to wander: maybe we are all too affluent nowadays. It is good to hear the high-pitched and somewhat tuneless renderings of familiar carols outside our homes on a winter's evening. It would be sad if these youthful, informal groups of singers were entirely replaced by large, organised and well-rehearsed adult choirs.

Mummers, or *"guisers"* also went from house to house during the weeks preceding Christmas and, in some areas, through to New Year. These figures were dressed up in weird costumes which were covered in fluttering strips of material or paper; originally the costumes would have been decorated with fluttering green leaves to represent spring and fertility; centuries later these green leaves became translated into material strips or ribbons.

The Green Man, or Jack O' the Green, seen so often on church bosses and carvings, was this same spirit of springtime and fecundity; he too was clothed all in *"greenery"*.

Often the characters were masked, or *"disguised"*, hence the title *"guisers"*, and in some areas the actors would blacken their faces to effect a disguise. The original players in these rustic performances performed entirely in mime, and some authorities believe the word *"Mummer"* derives from the old French word *"MOMER"*, meaning to act in dumb show. Our expressions to *"keep mum"*, or silent, about a subject also comes from this word. Alternatively, certain scholars think the word comes from the German *"MUMMEN"*, meaning mask, and yet another school of thought favours the Greek *"MOMME"*, the word for a frightening mask or bogey-man. The origins of these ancient plays are so lost in the mists of time that we will probably never know for certain how the name originated. Mummer's plays have been performed since Celtic times during the dark, long days of winter, for they traditionally embody the triumph of spring over winter, fertility returning to the barren land and light overcoming darkness. The names of characters changed through time, and by the Middle Ages, when knights went off to fight in the Crusades, goodness became identified with Saint George, and evil was portrayed by a Turkish knight, or Saracen. Saint George, who originated from Asia Minor, and is said to have been a Roman soldier, became a popular saint with the Crusaders, probably because they could more easily identify with this *macho* figure, and he eventually replaced Edward the Confessor as England's patron saint during the reign of Edward III in the fourteenth century. Important characters essential to Mummers' plays include the doctor or healer, who resurrected the slain Turkish Knight, with the help of Bold Slasher, Saint George, Beelzebub, Jack Finney, and often Old Father Christmas, who must not be confused with the modern Santa Claus. He is thought to have originated from the Nordic god Odin, who was believed to roam the northern hemisphere during the dark days of the winter solstice disguised as an old man in a hood and cloak so that he could distribute gifts to the deserving and needy. In addition to these characters many regional variations exist.

Ritual combat is an essential part of these plays, and rustic actors throughout the centuries have much enjoyed the rough and tumble entailed in the re-enactment of these naïve plays.

In 1348 Edward III was entertained at Christmastide by;

"two hundred mummers eighty of whom were in buckram, many others in visaurs (visors) depicting women, bearded men, and angels, while some mounted dragons, peacocks or swans. They wore tunics embroidered with gold and silver stars".

Thomas Hardy wrote about Mummers making their rounds in the nineteenth century West Country. In *"The Return of the Native"* he vividly describes their fluttering costumes and masks, and in *"Under the Greenwood Tree"* and *"Life's Little Ironies"* he gives us a wonderful description of a village band doing their valiant best to perform in a freezingly cold village church at Christmas time and traipsing about the countryside singing carols.

These ancient plays are not special to Britain, as there are similar forms of plays throughout Europe; indeed some nine hundred existing variations have been recorded.

The Mummers often completed their performances with a local carol and received alms and refreshments in reward for their entertainment. Apart from very occasional visits by troupes of itinerant actors, the Mummers were the only form of live theatre experienced by most rural communities during past times. In these days of television, radio and theatre it is hard for us to imagine the impact that these simple playlets made upon ordinary people. Ancient rituals became forgotten, but the fun and entertainment remained to be enjoyed every Yuletide.

Deck the halls with boughs and holly,
'tis the season to be jolly,
Don we now our gay apparel,
Troll the ancient Yule-tide carol.

See the blazing Yule before us,
Strike the harp and hear the chorus,
Follow me in merry measure,
While I tell of Yule-tide treasure.

Fast away the old year passes,
Hail the new, ye lads and lasses,
Sing we joyous all together,
Heedless of the wind and weather.

A Traditional Welsh carol used for dancing, often to a harp accompaniment.

One of our most treasured modern traditions is the Festival of Nine Lessons and Carols which takes place annually, on Christmas Eve, at King's College Cambridge, from there it is broadcast all over the world. It did not however have its beginnings in Cambridge. In 1880 The Rt: Rev: Edward White Benson, Bishop of Truro, who later became Archbishop of Canterbury, began this most famous of carol services in a wooden hut as Truro Cathedral was, at that time, under construction. The original purpose of the service was said to have been an event which would help to keep the local men out of the pubs on Christmas Eve and to discourage drunkenness. I think they must have needed a very large shed to accomplish this objective! Later the service was adopted by King's College in 1918 and first broadcast by the BBC in 1928. King's College Chapel has a choir consisting of sixteen trebles as specified in the statutes laid down by Henry VI, its founder. Fourteen undergraduates from King's College, Cambridge sing the men's parts, though in the past choral scholars and lay clerks performed this office.

For British people living abroad this Christmas Eve Festival, broadcast by the BBC World Service, is a very real link with Christmas "at home". Whilst living in Turkey, I listened to the Festival of Nine Lessons and Carols on Christmas Eve with a lump in my throat and experienced an overwhelming sense of homesickness for my native land and the English Christmas I knew and loved.

Great numbers of people attend similar services close to Christmas in their own churches and local cathedrals. For many of us Christmas truly begins with those first magical notes of "Once in royal David's city" floating across the darkened church amidst the flickering candles. It is a truly heavenly sound ushering in all that is best in the Christmas season.

With the Compliments of the Season

*O*ur compliments and thanks to you all. For it is thanks very largely to you for so loyally and so helpfully working with us that at this, the fourth Christmas at war, the nation's health is on a sound footing. But though "good living" must now be taken in the sense of healthy living, instead of luxury living, and we all must go carefully with fuel, we can still make Christmas fare hearty, appetising and tempting to look at. Here, with our very best wishes, are some ideas which may help you:

■ Christmas Day Pudding

Rub 3 oz. cooking fat into 3 tablespoonfuls self-raising flour until like fine crumbs. Mix in 1½ breakfastcupfuls stale breadcrumbs, ½ lb. prunes (soaked 24 hours, stoned, chopped) or any other dried fruit such as sultanas, 3 oz. sugar, 1 teaspoonful mixed spice, ½ teaspoonful grated nutmeg. Then chop 1 large apple finely, grate 1 large raw carrot and 1 large raw potato; add to dry ingredients. Stir in a tablespoonful lemon substitute. Mix 1 teaspoonful bicarbonate of soda in 3 tablespoonfuls warm milk and stir thoroughly into pudding mixture. Put into one large or two small well-greased basins, cover with margarine papers and steam for 2½ hours. This can be prepared overnight and cooked on Christmas Day.

■ Emergency Cream

Bring ⅛ pint water to blood heat, melt 1 tablespoonful unsalted margarine in it. Sprinkle 3 heaped tablespoonfuls household milk powder into this, beat well, then whisk thoroughly. Add 1 teaspoonful sugar and ¼ teaspoonful vanilla. Leave to get very cold.

■ Christmas Fruit Pies

This mixture is a good alternative to mincemeat.

Warm 1 tablespoonful marmalade (or jam, but this is not so spicy) in small saucepan over tiny heat. Add ¼ lb. prunes (soaked 24 hours, stoned, chopped) or other dried fruit, 1 tablespoonful sugar, 1 teacupful stale cake crumbs, or half cake, half breadcrumbs, ½ teaspoonful mixed spice. Stir together until crumbs are quite moist. Remove from heat, add 1 large chopped apple; also some chopped nuts if you have any. Make up into small pies, or large open flans. The mixture keeps several days in a cool place.

■ Stuffed Mutton *With apple or bread sauce, this is as delicious as any turkey!*

1 leg of mutton, or loin of mutton (half a leg does, but is more difficult to stuff). Bone with a sharp carving knife and small kitchen knife, or get your butcher to do it. Spread the meat flat, stuff one end with your favourite savoury stuffing, one end with sausage meat, the two meeting in the centre. Fold meat over, re-forming into shape, sew with sacking-needle and stout thread, place seam side down in baking dish, spread liberally with dripping. Put halved potatoes, peeled or in jackets, in the baking dish. Allow about 40-50 minutes before joint is done.

ISSUED BY THE MINISTRY OF FOOD (S50)

* Don't waste elsewhere the fuel you save at home.

World War II festive economy recipes issued by the Ministry of Food 1942-45

12

CHRISTMAS FARE

"We all want some figgy pudding,
We all want some figgy pudding,
We all want some figgy pudding,
*   so bring some out here!*

We won't go until we get some,
We won't go until we get some,
We won't go until we get some,
*   so bring some out here!"*

(Part of a traditional Mummer's Carol)

CHRISTMAS PUDDINGS

Stir-Up Sunday falls on the Sunday before Advent and five weeks before Christmas. Porridge Sunday was a more colloquial term given to it by country wags. Stir-Up Sunday gets its name from the Collect for that day in the English Book of Common Prayer:

"Stir up we beseech Thee, O Lord, the wills of thy faithful people, that they plenteously bringing forth the fruit of good works, may of Thee be plenteously rewarded".

These words seemed to have acted as a reminder to housewives that it was time to mix, boil, and store away their puddings, mincemeat, etc., in readiness for the coming Christmas feast. Christmas cakes would have been made some time previously, usually about October, so that they could mature into the moist, rich cake eaten at our festivities.

The earliest form of Christmas Pudding was plum porridge, or plum pottage, which was a mixture of oats, brown bread, spices and dried fruits, especially figs and prunes; an essential ingredient was meat which was gradually discontinued through the centuries.

Below is an original eighteenth century recipe for Plum Pottage by a Mrs. MacIver.

"Take a hough of beef and a knuckle of neat (ox), put them on a fire in a close pot, with six or seven pints of water; take out the neat before it is over boiled, and let the beef boil till the whole substance is out of it; strain off the stock, and then put in the crumbs of a two-penny loaf, two pounds of currants well cleaned, two pounds of rasins ston'd, and one pound of prunes. Let all boil together till they swell; then warm the neat and put it in the middle of the dish."

Quite often sugar or honey, sack (sherry) and spices such as cloves, nutmeg and mace were added to the mixture forming a type of sweet and sour dish.

As late as 1801, the scholar and antiquary William Brand wrote:

"I dined at the chaplain's table at St. James' on Christmas Day and partook of the first thing served and eaten on that festival at the table, i.e. a tureen full of rich luscious plum-porridge. I do not know that the custom is anywhere else retained".

By the early nineteenth century plum pudding had overtaken plum porridge in popularity. The meat had, by then, become a discontinued ingredient, but of course, chopped beef suet remained, as did the bread, fruits, spices and alcohol. Interestingly, the Romans made a very similar pudding to our traditional Christmas pudding and below is the recipe recorded by Herodotus.

"Prepare and mix in the usual manner one pound of fine raisins, stoned, one pound of minced beef suet, half a pound of breadcrumbs, four figs chopped small, two tablespoons of honey, two wineglasses of wine (sherry) and the rind of half a large lemon, grated. Boil the pudding for fourteen hours."

The cooking time seems somewhat lengthy but I'm sure the recipe would yield a pudding worthy of our modern festive board. Traditionally puddings were boiled in floured cloths, often, if the family was large, in the copper normally used for boiling the weekly wash. Dickens must have been familiar with the sight of the Victorian housewife heaving out her giant pudding for he writes in *"A Christmas Carol"*:

"Mrs. Cratchit left the room alone - too nervous to bear witnesses - to take the pudding up and bring it in. Suppose it should not be done enough! Suppose it should break in turning out! Suppose somebody should have got over the wall of the back-yard, and stolen it, while they were merry with the goose - a supposition at which the two young Cratchits became livid! All sorts of horrors were supposed. Hallo! A great deal of steam! The pudding was out of the copper. A smell like a washing-day! That was the cloth. A smell like an eating house and a pastrycook's next door to each other, with a laundress's next door to that! That was the pudding! In half a minute Mrs. Cratchit entered - flushed, but smiling proudly - with the pudding, like a speckled cannon-ball, so hard and firm, blazing in half of half-a-quarter of ignited brandy, and bedight with Christmas holly stuck into the top.

Oh, a wonderful pudding! Bob Cratchit said, and calmly too, that he regarded it as the greatest success achieved by Mrs. Cratchit since their marriage. Mrs. Cratchit said that now the weight was off her mind, she would confess she had had her doubts about the quantity of flour. Everybody had something to say about it, but nobody said or thought it was at all a small pudding for a large family. It would have been flat heresy to do so. Any Cratchit would have blushed to hint at such a thing."

Mrs Cratchit lifts out her Christmas pudding - by R.Seymour (1798-1836)

In Medieval and Tudor times dried fruits and spices were the prerogative of the rich as, coming from the eastern countries, they were both scarce and very expensive, being a luxury to indulge in during the Christmastide celebrations. Most poor people would never have tasted such delicacies - indeed, even meat was considered to be a treat.

During the 1914-18 war and again during the Second World War ingredients for Christmas Puddings became scarce or more often completely unobtainable. An austerity pudding became a necessity and the Ministry of Food issued the recipes for use during the somewhat un-festive season of 1942 using whatever ingredients happened to be available to the housewife. Many older people remember the wartime Christmas Pudding, and recall how very good it was especially if the precious dried fruit ration had been carefully hoarded for months before so that the pudding was extra fruity and flavoursome on The Day! A recipe for wartime mincemeat was also included - how inventive we were with the few ingredients we had to hand.

Traditionally plum pudding was served with wine sauce or later, brandy or rum sauce, which were basically good sweetened egg or white sauces to which the alcohol was added. During recent times brandy butter seems to be the favoured accompaniment, but this is often very rich and greasy when added to an already rich pudding; the pouring sauces, which used to be poured right over the puddings on serving, were much lighter and thus, a better balance in taste was achieved with the Christmas pudding. The whole succulent dripping pudding was surmounted by a choice piece of berried holly symbolising everlasting life.

> *Yule! Yule!*
> *Three puddings in a pool*
> *Crack nuts and cry Yule!*

It is considered lucky for the whole family in turn to make a wish whilst stirring the Christmas pudding before it is cooked. Often included in the pudding would be little silver charms which each held a special message or symbol; the button for bachelor or spinsterhood, a bell foretold marriage, a horse shoe for good luck, an anchor denoted travel, a donkey, well, that needs no explanation!

These little charms are fun, but dangerous to the unwary eater.

In Victorian times a tiny silver threepenny bit called a "joey" was placed in the pudding and later the sixpenny piece took its place. After decimalisation a fivepence or tenpence piece, which is wrapped in foil because it no longer contains silver, has become the usual coin included for good luck. The introduction recently of the small fivepence pieces, which are very similar in size to the old "joeys", seem to have brought this custom round again, full circle. In the past, a whole almond would be placed in the plum porridge ensuring the finder good luck throughout the coming year. In Scandinavia the custom is still adhered to except that the pudding is creamy rice, with raisins and spices. The mixture is much closer to our original plum porridge and does not appear to have evolved into a solid pudding, as in Britain.

Flaming the Christmas pudding with warmed, ignited brandy is still popular. Little do people realise that this too is a pagan practice symbolising the return of the sun bringing with it warmth and fertility to the land during the ensuing spring months. When the housewife enters the dining room bearing her blazing Yuletide pudding she is indeed the great high-priestess of the festive board.

The Christmas Pudding

Into the basin
put the plums,
Stir-about, stir-about,
stir-about!

Next the good
white flour comes,
Stir-about, stir-about,
stir-about!

Sugar and peel
and eggs and spice,
Stir-about, stir-about,
stir-about!

*Mix them and fix them
and cook them twice,
Stir-about, stir-about,
stir-about!*

Anon

MINCE PIES

*Dame get up and bake your pies
On Christmas Day, on Christmas Day.
Dame get up and bake your pies
On Christmas Day in the morning.*

Traditional rhyme

Mincemeat was just that not so long ago, for it comprised of a mixture of minced lean beef, mutton or neat's (ox) tongue, dried fruits, apples, suet, honey, spices and alcohol. Gradually the meat disappeared and we were left with the mixture which is so familiar to us today. Parts of America still include meat in their recipes which were handed down to them by their early settler ancestors.

Robert Herrick, the poet (1591 – 1674) writes about this old recipe for mince pies.

*Drink now the strong Beere,
Cut the white loafe here,
The while the meat is a-shredding;
For the rare Mince-Pie
And the plums stand by
To fill the paste that's a-kneading.*

We are now very familiar with the small individually sized pies but this is not the traditional way to bake them and in any case they tend to be 70% pastry and only 30% filling. In the olden days pies, or *"coffins"*, were large, open, and usually oval in shape, thus representing the manger in which Christ was placed after his birth. Often the sides were marked with a fork and a criss-cross pattern of pastry strips was placed over the top of the rich filling, thus simulating the weave of wattle or cane-work. A tiny pastry Christ-child used to be placed on the top of the pies. The Puritans banned these large pies with their alcoholic filling and representation of the Christ Child, as being heathen and Popish, but they returned with the Restoration of Charles 11.

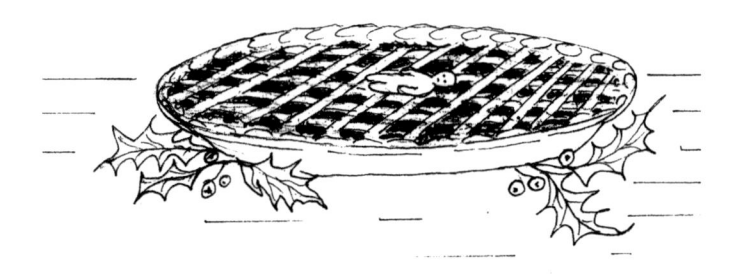

Large pies are easily made on round metal baking plates and are so much more succulent than the small variety. They can be open or enclosed with a pastry topping. Puff pastry rather than short pastry used to be the favourite paste in the past. Just see peoples faces light up when they taste these plate pies especially if the mincemeat is homemade and well laced with brandy or rum. Some people serve their warm mince-pies with brandy butter, but this can make them rather sickly.

Originally brandy or rum butter was served on plain crackers or shortbread biscuits and it is very delicious when used in this way. An old Cumberland recipe goes as follows:

"2lb of <u>best</u> pale soft Barbados, 1lb. fresh soft unsalted butter, 2 small glasses rum, cinnamon and freshly grated nutmeg to taste". 1) Beat the butter up with your hand. 2) Beat in the sugar, then the rum, nutmeg and cinnamon. 3) Put into a large jar or basin

and smooth the top. On no account must it have a rough or rocky appearance."

American Hard Sauce is very similar to this. Of course these quantities are somewhat large for a modern household but it will keep for a long time if well covered and stored in a cool place, preferably a refrigerator. Nowadays a food mixer could be used for blending the ingredients together.

Rum butter is sometimes called "Sweet Butter". A bowl of it used to be prepared in readiness for the coming of a new baby to a family. Visitors coming to see the new infant were offered some on biscuits. A tiny piece of this "Sweet Butter" was placed in the baby's mouth as its first taste of earthly food.

It is said that for every mince pie you eat during the twelve days of Christmas you will have a lucky month. It would seem that tradition says the greedier you are the more fortunate you are likely to be in the coming year! On eating the first mince pie of the Christmas season you should make a wish - perhaps for a strong digestive system during the ensuing feast.

> *"Little Jack Horner*
> *Sat in the corner,*
> *Eating his Christmas Pie;*
> *He put in his thumb,*
> *And pulled out a plum*
> *And said what a good boy am I!"*

We are all familiar with this old nursery rhyme from our infancy, but perhaps many people do not realise that Jack Horner was a real person. He lived during the reign of Henry VIII and was steward to the last Abbot of Glastonbury, one of the richest monasteries in England. At the time of the Dissolution of the monasteries, Abbot Whiting sent a large Christmas pie packed with the title deeds of twelve manors belonging to the monastery as a gift to the King, hoping that this very generous bribe would postpone the destruction of his Abbey. Jack Horner was entrusted with the delivery of this Christmas pie with its unusual filling. He was, however, able to extract the deeds to the manor of Mells in Somerset which he hid until after the irrevocable closure of Glastonbury Abbey, and later produced them claiming his right to the property. He and his descendants managed to enjoy his questionable acquisition of these lands, but the rhyme shows that his actions did not go un-noticed by his contemporaries.

> *Then hey for Christmas once a year*
> *When we have cakes, with ale and beer,*
> *For at Christmas every day*
> *Young men and maids may dance away.*

Anon 16th Century

CHRISTMAS CAKE

> *"The Yule cake dotted thick wi' plumbs*
> *Is on each supper table found,*
> *And cats look up for falling crumbs*
> *Which greedy children litter round."*

Shepherds Calendar 1827. John Clare.

Christmas cake used to be a Twelfth Night cake eaten on the final night of the Christmas festivities. Unfortunately this custom has lapsed and now we eat it during tea-time on Christmas Day, when most people are too full to enjoy it properly. Until late Victorian times bakers would prepare and ice elaborately decorated cakes often depicting whole scenes with tiny figures made out of icing sugar. It was the custom to walk along the streets just before Twelfth Night and look at all the wonderful confections made by the local bakers and displayed in their illuminated windows. Many of the themes were not particularly "Christmassy" but could be pastoral, floral, or themes taken from well known stories etc.

As far back as medieval times cakes formed an integral part of the Yuletide and New Year feasting. Often they were made into elaborate models of castles, ships, animals etc. by means of moulded, shaped "marchpane", or marzipan as we call it today. These lavishly decorated confections were known as "subtleties" and placed in positions of honour on the festive board.

These Twelfth Night cakes contained a whole dried bean or pea; the lucky man who found the bean was made "king" until the stroke of midnight, and whichever lady found the pea was made his "queen". Sometimes a lady found the bean and the man a pea in which case they selected the "king" or "queen" of their choice. During their reign they could command anyone to do any task or forfeit and even the real monarch had to obey or be thought a spoil sport by the assembled company.

Usually the forfeits were slight foolish things such as we have today but occasionally people were able to pay back old scores against their enemies, It is recorded that Henry VIII was not at all amused when commanded by his Twelfth Night rival to perform a forfeit. In 1563 when Mary Queen of Scots was spending Christmas at Holyrood Palace near Edinburgh, her lady-in-waiting, Mary Fleming, found the lucky bean in her portion of cake and was made "queen" for the rest of the day wearing, we are told, the real Queen's own clothes. Our expression "having a bean feast" meaning a jolly good party comes from this custom.

The French say *"Il trouvé la fève au gâteau"* - *"He has found a bean in his cake"*- when they wish to say someone has had good luck. This old custom must have caused much fun and hilarity during the final Twelfth Night celebrations no matter whether they were enjoyed in the King's palace or a cottager's humble abode.

Again, Robert Herrick wrote a poem in the seventeenth century describing this ritual.

> *"Now, now the mirth comes*
> *With cake full of plums*
> *Where Beane's the King of Sport here;*

Beside we must know,
The Pea also
Must revell, as Queene, in the court here."

Twelfe Night

Robert Baddeley must have enjoyed his Twelfth Night cake for he left an instruction in his will of 1795 that a sum of money should be set aside to *"...provide cake and wine for the performers in the green room of Drury Lane on Twelfth Night".* Happily this tradition is continued and enjoyed by the actors and theatre staff up to the present day. Needless to say a toast is drunk to the memory of Robert Baddeley. Before becoming an actor he was a confectioner and pastry cook and must have made many cakes himself in celebration of Twelfth Night.

An old recipe, or receipt for *plumb cake* and dated 1718 goes as follows:

"Half a quarten of flouer 3 quarters of a pound of Butter a little salt 4 eggs, half a nutmeg a little genger 3 or 4 spoonfuls of yeast 2 of Brandy 2 of white wine. Mix it up with warm milk 3 quarters of a pound of currains, half a pound of Loaf sugar".

This recipe would have produced a rich, spicy type of currant bread whilst modern recipes have dropped the yeast in favour of a raising agent in the flour.

Wartime Britain meant economies and shortages but not the total abandonment of the Christmas cake. There is an austerity cake recipe issued by the Ministry of Food in 1945, using soya bean flour and artificial almond flavouring for the "marzipan" icing, and the inclusion of dried eggs sent to Britain by the Americans during World War II.

Christmas Cake with Holly Leaf Icing

THE CAKE : 4 oz. sugar, 4 oz. margarine, 1 tablespoon syrup, 8 oz. flour, 2 level teaspoons baking powder, 1 level teaspoon cinnamon, 1 level teaspoon mixed spice, 2-4 eggs (reconstituted), 1 lb. mixed fruit, ½ teaspoon lemon substitute, pinch of salt, milk to mix (about 1/8 pint).

Cream sugar and margarine, add syrup. Mix flour, baking powder, salt and spices together. Add alternately with the egg to the creamed mixture and beat well. Add fruit and lemon substitute and enough milk to make a fairly soft dough. Line a 7-in. tin with greased paper, put in the mixture, and bake in a moderate oven for two hours.

HOLLY LEAF ICING : For this you will need : 4 oz. soya flour, 2 oz. margarine, 2 oz. sugar, 4 tablespoons water, almond essence to taste, few drops of green and red cookery colouring.

Melt margarine and water together, stir in the sugar, then the essence. Divide about a quarter of the resulting liquid into two cups; a little more in one than the other, and keep warm. Stir about three-quarters of the soya flour into the bulk of the liquid, turn out, knead the paste thoroughly, pat to about 1/8th thick, press on top of cake and neaten edges. Put a drop or two green colouring into cup holding most liquid, stir in flour and treat as for plain paste. Cut into leaf shapes, mark veins with knife, pinch round edges to form "prickles." Put red colouring into other cup, treat as before, form red paste into tiny balls. Arrange leaves and berries on top of cake in wreath shape or sprays, as you fancy.

ISSUED BY THE MF MINISTRY OF FOOD

(S135)

Nowadays the shops are full of delicious ready-made and decorated cakes. Many housewives have given up the tradition of baking their own cakes but nothing can replace the delicious smell of a slowly cooking spiced cake wafting around the house. It is the smell of Christmas.

The Christmas Cake

Mix the cake, mix the cake,
Stir it round and round,
Spices by the ounce and
currants by the pound.

Stir the cake, stir the cake,
Make it rich and spicey
Add the eggs, beat it up
That will do quite nicely.

Bake the cake, bake the cake
Till it's cooked and brown,
There it is, yours and mine
The very best cake in town.

Eat the cake, eat the cake,
Enjoy it right away,
Eat up every single crumb
For today is Christmas day.

          Monica Evans

13

TURKEYS, GEESE and CHRISTMAS MEATS

"Departed goose!....
We pronounce thee fine,
Season'd with sage, onions, and port wine".
                                Robert Southey. 1774 - 1843

"Capons and Hennes, besides Turkies, Geese and Duckes, besides Beefe and Mutton, must all die for the great feast, for in twelve days a multitude of people will not be fed with little......Christmas is a costly purveyor of excess".
                                Nicholas Breton 1625

Turkey has become synonymous with Christmas. It has not always been so however, as these birds are comparative newcomers to our Christmas table. They originated in the Americas, and not the country of Turkey as may be thought; it seems that the early discoverers of the New World thought that they had landed in the

East and so named the bird, which was much enjoyed by the local native American Indians. The Spaniards brought this large bird to Europe in 1527 and it was introduced into Britain some years later. Henry VIII is the first British monarch known to have eaten turkey at a Christmas feast.

Only since Victorian times has it become readily available to the public at large, although a few were enjoyed by rich people from the sixteenth century onwards.

A variety of birds, game and meats were served at important medieval banquets including swans and peacocks which were served after roasting, dressed and adorned by their own feathers. They were probably more spectacular than edible.

The most popular bird eaten at our Christmas feasts years ago was the goose. Legend has it that Elizabeth I decreed that goose should be served at Christmas after receiving news of the final destruction of the Spanish Armada during a feast at which she happened to be eating roast goose.

Lincolnshire and Norfolk were especially well known for the breeding of geese. In those far off days there was no refrigeration or swift transportation by road and rail. The geese, therefore, had to be walked to market. It must have been a marvellous sight to see hundreds of geese being driven across country to the large towns and cities by the drovers during the weeks preceding Christmas. It was a journey that took days and often weeks. The birds were fed en route and they roosted by the wayside at night, being guarded from foxes and thieves by the drovers who slept alongside them in the fields and hedgerows. Their wings were clipped to prevent them flying away. Because of the lengthy walk many of the geese suffered from sore and blistered feet and so a special remedy was affected to prevent this happening. A tub of tar or pitch was heated up and each goose had its webbed feet quickly dipped into the warm mixture. Afterwards they were stood onto a pile of sand so that it bonded with the tar forming "soles" on the feet of the geese. Turkeys were also "shod" in this way. What a comical sight it must have been to see all those geese in their black "wellies" waddling down the country lanes.

Poor people often paid into Goose Clubs throughout the year, depositing a penny or two at a time from their precious wages. With the arrival of the Christmas holiday week, or the full twelve days during early times, all pay ceased. Paid holidays were unknown until very recently; no work, no pay was the general rule, and so it became essential for working people to save for their Christmas treats in advance. The Goose Clubs were often run and organised by local public houses and just before Christmas the great draw took place; the bars were crowded to capacity and a great deal of fun, not to mention drinking, ensued. A name would be pulled from a bag or hat and the owner would be given first choice of bird; this went on until all the birds were gone. The geese had to be carefully locked away as it was not unknown for them to disappear overnight prior to the Goose Club draw.

Birds and animals were not slaughtered until just before Christmas because of the difficulty of keeping the meat fresh for any length of time. Butchers bought the animals live on the hoof - or wing - and most of them had their own slaughter yards at the back of their shops where the animals were fed, rested and kept until needed and then they were slaughtered, the carcass being dressed by the butcher himself. Old pictures show butchers' shops displaying fantastic arrangements of flesh, fowl and game during the festive season.

Unsold birds and meat would often be sold off cheaply late on Christmas Eve. Shops stayed open until very late in those days and the shop assistants worked long hours in the bitterly cold conditions. A brisk trade was often done late on Christmas Eve with late night shoppers seeking a bargain, and this arrangement often helped the poorer section of the community to procure a reasonably priced Christmas dinner.

It was the custom, especially in rural communities, for Christmas goose, turkey, capon or joint to be taken down to the local bakery ready prepared in a baking tin, so that they could be baked there in the large oven for the price of a penny or so. Few poor people possessed an oven or the means to fuel it and so whole communities had their birds and meat cooked en masse. There are still old people who remember the birds being taken along to the bakehouse in this way during their childhood. It was quite a sensible arrrangement as fuel to fire a hot oven was expensive and the baker's ovens were already hot from the early morning baking of bread. The birds and joints were collected just before the meal was ready to be served; dozens of people would be seen hurrying along with their tins covered by cloths to keep the meat warm.

Sage and onion stuffing has always accompanied goose in English cookery, and often a gooseberry sauce, hence its name, or an apple sauce. These sharp fruity sauces counteracted the greasiness of a roasted goose. Chestnut stuffing was used for turkeys; capons and other fowl had a parsley, thyme and lemon mixture.

Port wine sauce, or Dr. Hunter's Sauce, as it was known, became an essential accompaniment to goose during the nineteenth century. A recipe dated 1807 goes as follows:

"A table spoonful of made mustard. half a teaspoonful of Cayenne pepper, and three spoonsful of port wine. When mixed, pour this (hot) into the body of the goose, by a slit in the apron, just before sending it up....This is a secret worth knowing. It wonderfully improves sage and onion stuffing."

Alternatively, this sauce could be stirred into melted butter or thickened gravy and served up in a sauce boat as an accompaniment to the goose. Cumberland sauce and Sauce Robert were also popular during the Victorian era, particularly when served with roast turkey; also a white wine and oyster sauce poured over the bird just before serving became very fashionable at this time.

Roast turkeys often had links of sausages placed around their necks and breasts; a bird thus trimmed was known as an "Alderman in Chains". Old prints and Christmas cards often portray turkeys thus arrayed and they were a common sight right up to the turn of the ninteenth century.

Beef has always been popular in Britain and large joints were roasted at Yuletide. These joints were not the small portions we have today, but enormous ones; often a whole side of beef was roasted on a spit. The meat was made tender, moist and succulent by being basted at regular intervals in its own juices. Sirloin was a favourite cut and Charles II is said to have been so fond of this joint that he knighted it, hence Sir Loin! Some authorities believe it was James I who bestowed this honour upon his favourite Christmas meat; perhaps the love of beef ran in the family! The roast beef of Old England has been famous for many centuries, indeed Englishmen were sometimes called "Roastbeefs", particularly by the French.

Of course, the poor rarely saw these vast quantities of meat, but at Christmastide many landowners and lords of the local manors distributed gifts of meat and game to their tenants.

Thomas Tusser wrote in 1557;

> *"What season than better of the whole year,*
> *Thy needy poor neighbour to comfort and cheer...*
>
> *Provide us good cheer for thou knowest the old guise,*
> *Old customs that be good, let no man despise.*
> *At Christmas be merry and thank God of all,*
> *And feast thy poor neighbours, the great and the small."*

Seasonal hospitality and generosity was usually limited to a landowner's own tenants as abuses were otherwise likely to occur amongst the destitute vagrants who roamed the country, often through no fault of their own. Who can blame them for attempting to enjoy at least one good meal during the Christmas celebrations. In his Sketch Book, written during the early eighteen hundreds, Washington Irving, an American, makes note of the following event which took place at Bracebridge Hall during the Christmas festivities:

> *"The Squire went on to lament the deplorable decay of the games and amusements which were once prevalent at this season among the lower orders, and countenanced by the higher: when the old halls of castles and manor-houses were thrown open to daylight; when tables were covered with brawn and beef, and humming ale; when harp and carol resounded all daylong, and rich and poor were alike welcome to enter and make merry.....indeed, he had once attempted to put this doctrine into practice, and a few years before*

had kept open house during the holidays old style. The country people, however, did not understand how to play their parts in the scene of hospitality; many uncouth circumstances occurred; the manor was overrun by all the vagrants of the country, and more beggars drawn into the neighbourhood in one week than the parish officers could get rid of in a year. Since then he had contented himself with inviting the decent part of the neighbouring peasantry to call at the Hall on Christmas Day, and distributed beef, and bread, and ale among the poor, that they might make merry in their own dwellings."

Even at sea, the custom of Christmas feasting was observed and enjoyed as the following report from a seventeenth century English man-of-war testifies;

"Our captaine had all his officers and gentlemen to dinner with him, where wee had excellent good fayre; a rib of beife, plumb-puddings, minct pyes, etc., and plenty of good wines of several sorts; dranke healths to the King, to our wives and friends, and ended the day with much civill myrth"

Pork has always held an honoured place on our Christmas board. In early times, and right up to Tudor times, wild boar were hunted prior to Christmas and the carcasses were spit roasted as part of the Yuletide fare. The head was cooked separately and afterwards the tusks were gilded and the head was placed on a great dish which was decorated with rosemary, holly and bay. In its mouth was placed a large apple or orange, which is thought to have represented the sun. The parading of the Boar's Head was one of the highlights of a Christmas feast in days of yore.

It is undoubtedly true that the Boar's Head ceremony dates back to very ancient pre-Christian days. The Celts and Vikings venerated the wild boar and no doubt this ancient ceremony echoes some long forgotten rite of the Winter Solstice celebrations, possibly an animal sacrifice to the gods which was afterwards displayed before being eaten by the tribe. The Vikings ate wild boar at Jul and probably the hunting of it was partly ritualistic. To them it represented the Sun Boar, a great and powerful beast in their mythology. The heroes in the great hall of Valhalla were said to have feasted on boar's flesh, indeed they appear to have spent most of eternity eating and drinking! When wild boar became extinct in Britain, pigs heads replaced them.

The Boar's Head ceremony still takes place at Queen's College, Oxford, on the Saturday preceding Christmas, when the decorated head is carried in with due ceremony and pomp on a silver charger bedecked with greenery. The dish is held aloft whilst the accompanying choir herald its appearance with the Boar's Head Carol. Afterwards the head chorister is presented with the orange, a rare treat once, from its mouth and the assembled guests are given sprigs of rosemary, holly and bay.

The carol goes as follows:

> The boar's head in hand bear I,
> Bedecked with bays and rosemary,
> And I pray you, my masters, be merry,
> Quot estis in convivio.   (So many as are in the feast.)
> *Caput apri defero, (The boar's head I bring,)*
> *Redens laudes Domino, (Giving praises to God,)*
>
> The boar's head, as I understand,
> Is the rarest dish in all the land,
> Which thus bedecked with a gay garland,
> Let us servire cantico: (serve with a song)
> *Caput apri defero etc.*
>
> Our steward hath provided this,
> In honour of the King of bliss,
> Which on this day to be servéd is,
> In Reginensi atrio. (In the Queen's Hall.)
> *Caput apri defero etc.*

Traditional

The tune has again become well known and is sung on frequent occasions by choirs all over the country at Christmastide.

This ancient ceremony is, so legend has it, celebrated to commemorate the deliverance of a former Oxford student from a savage, wild boar whilst he was quietly walking and studying in nearby Shotover Forest. Not having any weapon to hand the young man thrust his volume of Aristotle down the creature's throat as it attempted to gore him, thus choking the creature. His college afterwards commemorated his brave deed annually at their Christmas feast.

This story must be taken with a very large pinch of salt, as it would seem that St.John's College and New College once had their own individual boar's head carols and ceremonies, and it is doubtful that they would have commemorated the deliverance of a student from a rival college.

The English court also had its boar's head feasts which were celebrated in colourful and elaborate style. In the twelfth century Henry II, had a boars-head served upon a great dish and accompanied by trumpets sounding a fanfare during a feast given to honour his son. Another cermony which took place at Christmas time during James I reign, was described as follows:

"The first messe (dish) was a Boar's Head which was carried by the tallest and lustiest of all the guard, before whom went one attired in a horseman's coat, with a boar's speare in his hande, next to him another Huntsman in greene, with a bloody faulcion (sword) drawn, next to him two Pages in tafatye sarcenet, (taffeta) each of them with a messe of mustard; next to whom came hee who carried the Boar's head crost with a green silke scarf, by which hunge the empty scabbard of the faulcion which was carried before him."

A quite different Boar's Head carol was sung on this occasion;

> The Boar is dead.
> Loe, here is his head,
> What man could have done more

Than his head off to strike,
Meleager like,
And bring it as I do before?
He livinge spoyled
Where good men toyled,
Which made king Ceres sorrye;
But now dead and drawn,
Is very good brawne
And we have brought it for you.
Then set down the Swineyard,
The foe of the Vineyard

Let Bacchus crown his fall,
Let this Boar's head and mustard
Stand for Pigg, goose and Custard,
And so you are wellcom all.

As can be seen from this old song English mustard with its fiery bite was a favourite accompaniment to this dish.

Brawn made from boiled and spiced pig's head was very popular amongst poorer people, probably because it made a little meat go a long way when prepared in such a manner. Often slices of this delicious brawn were served sprinkled with vinegar and a little brown sugar. Pork and game pies, often of great size, were popular on the festive board as indeed they still are.

The following article was published in the Newcastle Chronicle on January 6th 1770;

A Monster Dish

"Monday last was brought from Howick to Berwick, to be shipped to London, for Sir Henry Grey, Bart., a pie, the contents whereof are as follows:-

2 bushels of flour, 20lbs of butter, 4 geese, 2 turkies, 2 rabbits, 4 wild ducks, 2 woodcocks, 6 snipes, and 4 partridges, 2 neats' tongues, 2 curlews, 7 blackbirds, and 6 pidgeons; it is supposed a very great curiosity.

The pie was made by Mrs Dorothy Paterson, housekeeper at Howick.

It is nine feet in circumference at the bottom, weighs about twelve stones, and will take two men to present it to table; it is neatly fitted in a case with iron bands and four small wheels to facilitate its use to every guest that inclines to partake of its contents at table".

Sir Henry's guests must have been both amazed and delighted by the appearance of such a monstrous pie.

Both brawn and pork pie benefit from the traditional dish of English mustard, which cannot be successfully substituted by Continental mustards or pre-made varieties; the bite is just not there to give astringency to these pork dishes. Our ancestors knew how to complement one good dish with another.

Nowadays a greater variety of foods and meats are available to us than ever before, so that we may select whichever meat, bird, or even fish, that takes our fancy for the Christmas menu. Most people, however, choose one or even two from the traditional list. Long may we all continue to enjoy our festive board.

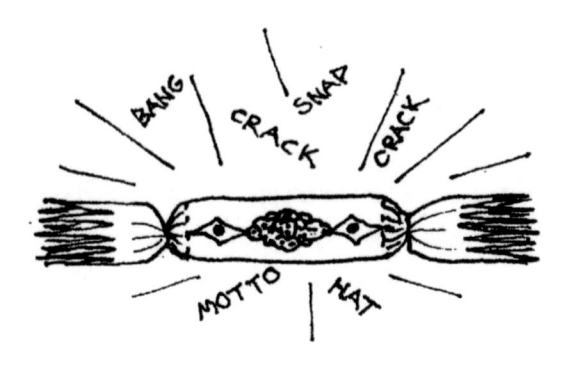

14

CRACKERS

With a crackle and snap! out falls the hat
To be placed on our heads with glee.
The mottoes so corny lie torn on the mat
Whilst we finish our Christmas Day tea.

Monica Evans

Crackers have played a part in our Christmas Day festivities since early Victorian times and so they are comparative newcomers to the Yuletide scene. Their inventor was Tom Smith. a successful confectioner, who had begun his career as a young boy assisting in the making and decorating of fanciful wedding cakes; being both inventive and industrious he experimented with, and developed new ideas and designs for cakes in his spare time. His confections became very popular with the clients of the shop and he decided to branch out on his own. Soon he had developed a thriving confectionary business and was able to travel abroad, where he was always on the look out for new and attractive ideas for his sweetmeats.

In 1840 he travelled to Paris, and there he saw bonbons on sale which were packed in twists of prettily patterned paper and decorated with lace and flowers. He decided to copy this idea in his own London shop and added little love mottoes as an extra attraction. Sales went reasonably well but he felt some extra novelty was needed to boost sales further. One cold winter's evening he was sitting by his fire and kicked a burning log with his toe to liven up the blaze. The log crackled and sent out a shower of sparks. Tom Smith thought how attractive this burning log was and developed the idea of packaging his sweets in log-shaped cylinders but still something was missing. The bang and crackle of a burning log seemed impossible to achieve. However, after much experimentation, Tom, and a friend who was a chemist, eventually succeeded in making a "snap" by chemically impregnating two strips of paper, which ignited by friction when the two strips were pulled apart. It was a bang-on idea!

Some cylinders covered in pretty papers were produced - these had frills at either end in order to contain and conceal the ends of the "snaps", and inside the cylinders were bonbons, mottoes, and often little gifts. He decided to market them under the name of "Cosaques" and later on "Crackers", and they became an immediate success. Later, paper-hats were included, and the early ones were very elaborate and quite substantial, being made of thick crepe paper and not at all like the thin tissue paper "crowns"which are included in our modern crackers.

"Love" or "kiss"mottoes continued to be popular for many years but gradually they were replaced by the jokes and riddles which we know today, indeed some of the jokes are still the original ones and have been illiciting both groans and laughter for several generations now.

A "love"motto dating from the 1890s went as follows:
"The sweet crimson rose with its beautiful hue
Is not half so deep as my passion for you.
Twill wither and fade, and no more will be seen,
But whilst my heart lives, you will still be its queen."

Many of these little verses were originally written by members of Tom Smith's staff and others were contributed by well known writers.

Tom Smith believed in advertising as the following words illustrate:

"*Thomas Smith and Company have endeavoured by employing special artists to produce designs, the finest modern appliances to interpret their work, and combining Art with Amusement and Fun with Refinement, to raise the degenerate cosaque from its low state of gaudiness and vulgarity to one of elegance and good taste.....the Mottoes, instead of the usual doggerel, are graceful and epigrammatic, having been specially written for Tom Smith's Crackers by well known Authors, among whom may be mentioned the late Thomas Hood, Esq., Charles H Ross, Esq.,Editor of Judy, Ernest Warren Esq., author of Four Flirts, Laughing Eyes etc."*

"Cosaques" or "cossacks" appears to have been the original name for crackers presumably because they sounded like the crackle of the cossack guns being fired by these dashing Russian troops. Contents of Victorian crackers were listed as follows:

"*Grotesque and Artistic Head dresses, Masks, Puzzles, Games, Conundrums. Jewels, Toys, Bric-a-brac, tiny treasures and Japanese Curiosities.*"

It would seem that the original crackers gave good value for money.

Crackers were made not just for the Christmas festivities but became popular decorative additions at weddings and other special occasions. Tom Smith's factory in Norwich, Norfolk, has a museum of old crackers and many of these have nothing to do with Christmas being both beautiful, fanciful and sometimes very sophisticated in design. Some lovely white lacy wedding crackers tied with lace and flowers still exist in this museum.

Today, this factory produces over two hundred crackers a minute and annually makes fifty-two million for export all over the world. Preparation for new crackers begins in the November of one year in order that the finished product shall be on the market ready for the following year's Christmas celebrations. Needless to say they are still the biggest manufacturer of crackers in the world.

In July 1998, Tom Smith's factory was bought out by a multi-national company who kept the original trade name of Tom Smith. Often, in the past, very large crackers were ordered and one of the most famous was made for use in a Victorian pantomime at Drury Lane. This enormous seven-foot cracker was pulled open by the comedian Tom Payne and a fellow actor; it contained change of costumes for both men and a multitude of small gifts enclosed in smaller crackers which were thrown out into the audience.

Another pantomime which was also produced at the Drury Lane Theatre in the nineteenth century, featured the famous clown and comedian Joseph Grimaldi, who entranced the audience by bursting out of a giant-like cracker whilst driving a tiny carriage pulled by a Shetland pony. On another occasion the little carriage was drawn by two large dogs. As Grimaldi drove across the stage he threw small gifts and bon-bons out to the delighted audience. It would be interesting to know if Tom Smith witnessed this theatrical event and that it possibly inspired his development of Christmas Crackers.

The title of "Joey" given to present day clowns originates from Joseph Grimaldi, who was the most famous clown and comedian of his day.

A six-foot cracker was made by Tom Smith's factory to decorate the entrance of Euston Station. Another cracker over eighteen feet long and containing gifts was produced for an important London banquet, and the assembled guests must have had great fun scrambling on the floor in all their finery in order to secure one of its treasures.

In 2002 the children of Ley Hill School in Chesham, Buckinghamshire, together with parents and helpers with the necessary expertise, produced a gigantic cracker, which at that time, claimed to be the largest in the world. In order to qualify for this prestigious title and be entered into the Guinness Book of Records certain rules had to be observed:

1) It had to look like a cracker.
2) A bang or crack was required when pulled apart.
3) It had to contain a hat, presents and a joke or motto.

The completed cracker was 207 feet (63.1metres) long, and 13 feet (4 metres) in diameter. It was made up from 650 feet (200metres) of 6"x2"(152 x 50mm) timber, half a mile of cardbroad, 1300 bolts, 1000 nails, 500 screws and half a mile of plastic tape. The construction took four days to erect.

The contents included 300 balloons, presents for the school children, a giant hat and a joke. It was pulled apart by 44 children and the Saracen's Rugby team to loud cheers from the local people. This spectacular feat raised money for the NSPCC, local schools and children with special needs.

Probably someone, somewhere, will in the future produce an even bigger and better cracker that is, if they have not succeeded in doing so already!

15

CRIBS

Neighbours, and is it really true,
True that the babe so small and new
  Is lying even now among us?
What can we lay upon his knees-
  He whose arrival angels sung us.
    What can we give,
What can we give the child to please?

Dickon shall bring a ball of silk,
Peter his son a pot of milk.
  And Tom a sparrow and a linnet,
Robin a cheese, and Ralph the half
  Part of a cake with cherries in it,
    And jolly Jack,
And jolly Jack a little calf.

I think this child will come to be
Some sort of workman such as we,
So he shall have my tools and chattels,
My well-set saw, my plane, my drill,
My hammer that so merry rattles,
And planks of wood,
And planks of wood to work at will.

When we have made our offerings,
Saying to him the little things
Whereof all babies born are witting,
Then we will take our leave and go,
Bidding goodnight in manner fitting-
Hush, hush, wee lamb,
Hush, Hush, wee lamb, dream sweetly so.

And in a stable though he lies,
We in our hearts will soon devise
Such mansions as can never shame him:
There we will house and hold him dear,
And through the world to all proclaim him:
'Wake up, good folk!
Wake up, good folk, for Christ is here.'

> Part of an old French carol
> "Voisin, d'où venait?" (Waking time).

According to the Oxford Dictionary a crib is a barred receptacle for cattle fodder; it can also mean a small bed for a child with barred sides, however, to most people, the word invokes the mental picture of the stable and the Christ Child lying within the hay-lined manger.

In the villages of Provence, *santons*, which are small figures representing various trades or professions, are placed around the images of the Holy Family which are displayed in their Christmas

Creche scenes. These used to have a prominent place in every Provencal village and can, to this day, still be seen in many rural areas of southern France.

The first crib was reputed to have been erected by Saint Francis of Assisi in a cave on the hillside above the Italian town of Grecchio on December 24th 1224. The Saint was overcome by a sense of love and wonder concerning Jesus' birth in the stable at Bethlehem. He decided to celebrate it by taking an ordinary manger or crib full of hay into the cave to symbolise the birthplace of Christ, and he prayed and worshipped before it with tears in his eyes. Later the idea was adopted by the local churches. At this stage it was an empty crib with no representation of the infant Jesus.

Saint Bonaventure, who lived during the thirteenth century and who became a leading Franciscan, ranking in authority and holiness only second to Saint Francis himself, describes how the original manger came to be arranged in time for the Christmas Eve mass:

"That this might not seem an innovation, he sought and obtained licence from the supreme pontiff, and then made ready a manger, and bade hay. together with an ox and an ass, be brought unto the place.... The man of God (Saint Francis), filled with tender love, stood before the manger, bathed in tears, and overflowing with joy. Solemn masses were celebrated over the manger, Francis, the Levite of Christ, chanting the Holy Gospel."

The word manger comes from the French "manger" meaning to eat. Before long this custom of taking a manger into the church on Christmas Eve had spread over much of Europe. Gradually it changed from the simple object before which Saint Francis worshipped to an elaborate arrangement containing a representation of the Christ Child, the animals present at His birth, though none were mentioned in the gospels, Mary His Mother, Joseph and, at a later date, the figures of the shepherds, the Wise Men, and often angels were also added. The stable itself was depicted and the figures placed within, sometimes they were life-size but more often in miniature such as we have in our churches today with the Star of Bethlehem shining above. Probably Saint Francis would be quite appalled by the cheap and shoddy plastic representations of the stable scene. A simple manger seems a much more appropriate and powerful symbol of the Nativity of Our Lord.

The figures of the shepherds are placed around the Holy Family on Christmas Eve and remain there until Twelfth Night when they are replaced by the figures of the Magi, or Wise Men, on January 6th, which is the Feast of the Epiphany (Greek: Epiphanea, which means the manifestation or showing of Christ to the world.) Kings are not mentioned in the Bible account of the Nativity and were a later interpretation by the establishment of the day. Neither is there a mention in the Bible of any specific number of Wise Men, although the gifts of gold, frankincense and myrrh suggest the number of three, and this is the usual group seen in cribs all over the world.

The figures of the Magi, sages or wise men in Greek, should remain in the crib until it is taken down at Candlemas on February 2nd.

In the olden days the hay which lined the crib was thought to have especially propitious and prophylactic qualities, and the populace used to fight for wisps and fragments on its removal from the church by the priests. People lucky enough to obtain a piece placed it in little leather bags hung around their necks in order to ward off illness and to bring them luck; sometimes it was placed on sick people to aid their cure, and often it was nailed onto the rafters of a house to protect it from evil. Barns and the animals which lived in them were thought to be protected from harm by pieces of this hay, which were placed above them in the timbers of the building.

Children, especially, love to look at the figures in the Christmas cribs. It is a pity that many are so shoddy and poor in design, bearing little resemblance to a real manger; perhaps though, it is the symbolism which counts most and the Star of Bethlehem continues to shine out from our hearts and eyes at Christmas time.

Cradle Song

Hush! my dear, lie still and slumber;
    Hush, Holy angels guard Thy bed!
Heav'nly blessings without number
    Gently falling on Thy head.

Soft and easy is Thy cradle;
    Course and hard thy Saviour lay!
When his birth-place was a stable
    And his softest bed was hay.

See the lovely Babe addressing;
    Lovely Infant how he smiled!
When he wept, the Mother's blessing
    Soothed and hushed the holy Child.

Lo, He slumbers in his manger,
    Where the horned oxen fed;
Peace my darling! here's no danger;
    Here's no ox a-near thy bed.

                        By Isaac Watts (1674-1748)

16

GIFTS

When Christmas comes about again,
O then I shall have money;
I'll hoard it up and box and all
I'll give it to my honey.

(18th Century anon.)

Seen from a Christian point of view, Christmas presents would appear to symbolise the gifts presented at the manger by the Magi, or Wise Men; gold represented kingship, frankincense symbolised divinity, and myrrh foretold suffering and death. It is only recently that gifts have been given universally to loved ones and friends at Christmas time; in the past the favoured period for gift giving was New Year. This probably originates from the Roman Kalends which began on January lst. at the Juvenalia (Feast of the Children) when strenae or gifts were given. The word strenae comes from the goddess of gift-giving and springtime growth, Strenia; her festival was held at this time and evergreen boughs were cut and placed on her shrine in the sacred groves. Christmas past was not specifically geared to children and few received gifts; however, as time passed by, various dates were introduced across Europe on which children were secretly presented with gifts by various donors, but not always the familiar Santa Claus.

The bringers of gifts range from the Star Boys of Poland to the Julnisse of Denmark, Saint Nicholas or Sinter Klass of Holland, to Father Frost of the modern USSR, Befana, the wandering woman of Italy, to the Christkind of Austria and Germany, and many others, including our own Father Christmas or Santa Claus. The dates on which gifts are delivered to the expectant and sleepless children vary from December 5th (St.Nicholas' Eve), December 6th (St.Nicholas' Day), and December 24th/25th to January 1st (New Year's Day), also January 5th (Epiphany Eve) and 6th (Epiphany), and January 7th in Russia.

It will be seen from the above dates that the actual day of gift-giving varies enormously from country to country. In medieval Britain, Childermass (Holy Innocents' Day on December 28th) was the most likely time for young children to be in receipt of a gift from fond parents or relatives. Children used to enjoy the privilege of playing inside churches on this day but it must have been a bitterly cold experience at this time of year. The festival commemorated the killing of the infant boys by Herod whilst he was attempting to find the Christ Child.

Gifts appear to have been given by tenants to landlords, and nobility to the sovereign, sometimes at Christmas, but more usually at New Year. It was also customary for tenants to receive gifts of meat, bread and ale from their employers or lords of the manor. Tradesmen sent gifts to valued customers (many complaining that it ate up their profits) and the sending of calendars to clients continues to this day in certain business establishments. Waits, carol singers and mummers were also the recipients of cash gifts and sometimes gifts in kind.

The establishment and the court at one time had a set rate of monetary gifts during the sixteenth and seventeenth centuries. During the reign of Elizabeth I an Archbishop could expect £40, peers £20, and the Sovereign £20. These gifts, or perks could be given in coin or plate, and usually the latter was preferred as it was more prestigious and valuable. Most sovereigns preferred personal gifts which outdid the peers' gifts in value and originality. Queen Elizabeth I made it quite plain to her courtiers that expensive personal gifts were expected at New Year. Some of the gifts listed included silk stockings, embroidered gloves, bejewelled ear-picks and tooth-picks, satin nightgowns, a sea-green satin petticoat, embroidered cushions and handkerchiefs, preserved glace fruits, sweetmeats (of which she was particularly fond), especially "marchpane" or marzipan, jewellery and perfume. Gloves seem to have been especially popular as New Year Gifts, and in 1627 Charles I received 70 pairs!

Most ordinary folk received gifts of food and, in turn, contributed comestibles towards the extremely generous gifts sent to the Lord of their particular area. Nicholas Breton (1626) advised his readers that they should *"...against new year provide for the presents."*

In 1636, Lord Chief Justice Bramston of Essex received the following gifts: 32 turkeys; 54 capons; 3 bullocks; many other birds; a hogshead of claret (52½ gallons); puddings; oysters and a basket of apples. Tenants and farmers gave capons and other smaller individual gifts; these tenants often had to walk or ride long distances in order to present their Christmas or New Year gifts and as a reward they received a small sum of money. His sister-on-law sent twenty turkeys; a neighbour gave a silver dish; Lord Petre and Mr.Darcy, a lawyer, each gave a dove. All these gifts were duly recorded in a "Christmas Book" which covered the period of the Twelve Days of Christmas which, of course, included New Year when most gifts were received. Lord Bramston does not appear to have lacked material things in this life.

Faithful and conscientious domestic servants could also expect a gift at this time of year from their masters and very often a large party was given for the entire household in great houses. This custom continued right up to the First World War.

Dr.Alianore Fairfax-Lucy of Charlecote in Warwickshire (which now belongs to the National Trust) recalled a Christmas in her youth when all the staff were entertained by the family (another instance of Yuletide role reversal).

"The entire staff, dressed in crisply starched aprons and pressed uniforms, sat down together to enjoy their annual Christmas treat. And the Fairfax-Lucy family, parents and children, served them their turkey and beef, with plum pudding and bread and cheese and, of course, with ale. When all were replete, they sat chatting; out came the clay pipes.....the children of the house washed up."

(Sally Rowat. Warwickshire & Worcestershire Life 1975)

On Christmas morning after church, during the Victorian and Edwardian eras, the tenantry of large estates often gathered around the enormous, glittering Christmas tree which had been placed in the great hall. The whole family would attend and usually the lady of the house gave a gift to every tenant and member of staff; very often their children also received presents. Gifts were such items as articles of clothing, foodstuffs and occasionally trinkets for the maidservants and of course the children received books or toys. Many former servants who used to work in the great houses of our land years ago still recall with great pleasure these Christmas gatherings, even though subservience was the order of the day and forelocks were touched with respect by menservants and a bob of a curtsey was required by the maids.

Boxing Day has nothing to do with the sport of boxing. It was the day on which alms boxes containing money for the poorer sections of the community were opened. Boxing Day falls on December 26th, or Saint Stephen's Day; he was the first known Christian martyr, and Saint Paul, who at that time was named Saul, is recorded in the Bible as being one of his persecutors: indeed we are told that he looked after the garments of the men who stoned Stephen to death.

The boxes were usually of pottery or wood with a built in slit at the top for receiving coins. The only way the contents could be taken out was to break open the box, rather like the familiar pottery pigs. No doubt some juggling with knives, etc., took place at times in order to extract the proceeds unofficially. A seventeenth century writer described these boxes in the following manner:

"A box having a cleft on the lid, or in the side, for money to enter it; used in France by begging Fryers, and here by Butlers, and Prentices etc."

Churches also had boxes which were of a more permanent nature in which alms were collected from parishioners and distributed to the poor and needy of the parish on Boxing Day. Coal, firewood and loaves of bread were often given to widows and paupers as well as money.

Tradesmen and service workers such as road-sweepers and dustmen were, until comparatively recent times, given gratuities on Boxing Day. Saint Wenceslas, if you remember, "stepped out" on this day to distribute his particular gifts of food, wine and fuel to the poor of his kingdom of Bohemia - now the Czech Republic - in the tenth century. He was a Christian king who was murdered by his pagan brother. A large statue of King Wenceslas now stands in the centre of Prague.

> Good King Wenceslas looked out
> On the Feast of Stephen,
> When the snow lay round about,
> Deep and crisp and even.
> Brightly shone the moon that night,
> Though the frost was cruel,
> When a poor man came in sight,
> Gath'ring winter fuel.
>
> "Hither, page, and stand by me,
> If thou know'st it telling,
> Yonder peasant who is he?
> Where and what his dwelling?"
> "Sire he lives a good league hence,
> Underneath the mountain,
> Right against the forest fence,
> By Saint Agnes fountain."

"Bring me flesh and bring me wine,
Bring me pine logs hither;
Thou and I will see him dine,
When we bear them hither".
Page and monarch forth they went,
Forth they went together;
Through the rude wind's wild lament,
And the bitter weather.

"Sire, the night is darker now,
And the wind blows stronger;
Fails my heart, I know not how,
I can go no longer."
"Mark my footsteps, good my page!
Tread thou in them boldly:
Thou shalt find the winter's rage
Freeze thy blood less coldly".

In his master's steps he trod,
Where the snow lay dinted;
Heat was in the very sod
Which the saint had printed.
Therefore Christian men be sure,
Wealth or rank possessing,
Ye who now will bless the poor
Shall yourselves find blessing.

In recent times Boxing Day has come to be connected with the various sporting events which now take place on the day following Christmas Day. Pantomimes also used to begin on this day, although many present day productions commence performances some time before the arrival of Christmas. Gift giving has always presented problems both to donors and recipients.

"What shall we give to so-and-so this year?" It is comforting to know that the Romans faced just such problems at their Feast of the Saturnalia. Martial, the Roman poet who lived in the first century, made the following comment:

> "You have sent me at the Saturnalia, Umber, all the presents you have collected in five days; twelve three-leaved tablets and seven tooth-picks, accompanied by a sponge; half a peck of beans; a wicker crate of Picenian olives, and a black flagon of Laletanian must: and with these some small Syrian figs, dried prunes, and a jar heavy with the weight of Libyan figs. I scarcely think the whole lot worth thirty sesterces, yet eight hulking Syrians carried it. How much more conveniently, and with no labour, might a boy have brought five pounds of silver plate!"

Unwanted gifts, it would appear, are no new phenomena.

The giving and receiving of gifts has always been an essential part of mankind's winter festivities and will, no doubt, continue to be so even if, at times, it becomes an exceedingly stressful practice which gets out of hand.

A Countrywoman's Tribute

What can I offer to a King newborn
From my poor store on this auspicious morn?
Only my jasmine gold to make His crown
And snowdrop silk to weave His swaddling gown.

No frankincense but my moss rose perfume
And clover flowers to scent his humble room.
No lustrous jewels but August's golden grain,
No spikenard-just gentle, healing rain.

A lark to praise Heaven for its precious Son,
Daffodil trumpets and a bluebell carillon.
A peacock's rainbow fan to cool His cheek,
Angel-winged dragonflies to guard His sleep.

A ball of cowslip bells for tiny hands to hold,
A fire of apple wood to beat the winter's cold-
What more can I give this King, of Kings apart?
With my small gifts I offer Him my heart.

                                                    Evelyn Knibbs

A charming poem written by a W.I. member shortly before she died from cancer.

17

LORDS of MISRULE, MASQUES and PANTOMIME

Well – come, my Lord, Christmasse
Well – come to us all:
Both more and lasse
Come near – Nowell!

All sudden, gorgeous hiss, and dragons glare
And ten-horn'd fiends and giants rush to war.
Hell rises, Heaven descends, and dance on earth
Gods, imps and monsters, music, rage and mirth,
A fire, a jig, a battle and a ball,
Till one wide conflagration swallows all.
Thence a new world to Nature's laws unknown,
Breaks out refulgent, with a heaven its own:
Another Cynthia, her new journey runs,

And other planets circle other suns.
The forests dance, the rivers upward rise,
Whales sport in woods, and dolphins in the skies;
And last, to give the whole creation grace,
Lo! One vast egg produces human race....*

Alexander Pope. 1688-1744.

Lords of Misrule were often chosen at All Hallows' Eve (October 31st) in olden times and their reign could last until Twelfth Night or, in medieval times, Candlemas (February 2nd) which, at that time, concluded the Christmas celebrations. It was not, however, unknown for them to continue their riotous rule right up to Shrove Tuesday and the onset of Lent.

Generally speaking, only the nobility and wealthy households could afford the luxury of a Lord of Misrule, whose task it was to ensure continuous and unalloyed merrymaking with spirited pastimes during the winter festivities.

Many sober citizens, and especially the Puritans, were outraged at some of the pranks indulged in by the Lord of Misrule and his attendants. In 1583, Phillip Stubbes wrote in his Anatomy of Abuses:

"The wildheads of the parish, conventing together, choose them a Grand-Captain (of all mischief) whom they ennoble with the title of my Lord of Misrule, and him they crown with great solemnity and adopt their king. This king anointed, chooseth forth twenty, forty, threescore or a hundred lusty guts, like to himself, to wait upon his lordly majesty, and to guard his noble person...Then march this heathen company towards the church and churchyard, their pipers piping, their drummers thundering, their stumps dancing, their bells jingling, their handkerchiefs swinging about their heads like madmen, their hobbyhorses and other monsters skirmishing amongst the throng; and in this sort they go to church (I say) and

---

*   Harlequin emerged from a huge egg in one eighteenth century pantomime.

into the church (though the Minister be at prayer or preaching), dancing and swinging their handkerchiefs...like devils incarnate with such a confused noise, that no man can hear his own voice. Then the foolish people they look, they stare, they laugh, they fleer, and mount upon forms and pews to see these goodly pageants solemnised in this sort."

The familiar carol "The Twelve Days of Christmas" seems to bear some similarity in certain verses to this description. Could it originally have derived from the merry disports of the Lord of Misrule and his rowdy cronies? Certainly the Morris Men appear to have been involved.

The Lord of Misrule reigned over the assembled company during the entertainments at court, issuing orders usually of a comical and ridiculous nature and often making the people present perform forfeits. Even the monarch had to obey his commands. It is recorded that Henry VIII was not at all amused when commanded by his Twelfth Night rival to perform a forfeit.

Lords of Misrule were also called Masters of Merry Disports, Masters of the Feast, Christmas Prince, Lords of Purpoole and probably many other similar but long forgotten titles. On December 27th. 1561, Henry Machyn described the following masque which was presented before Elizabeth I at the Temple in London:

"There came riding through London, a lord of misrule, in complete harness, gilt, with a hundred great horse and gentlemen riding gorgeously with chains of gold, and their horses goodly trapped unto the Temple, for there was great cheer all Christmas... and great revels as ever was for the gentlemen of the Temple every day."

The Bean King performed a similar service on Twelfth Night, indeed the roles of Lord of Misrule and the Bean King seem to have become indivisible and interchangeable, the only difference being that the Bean King and his consort were chosen on Twelfth Night at the final party of Christmastide when all the greenery was taken down and burnt.

These characters owe much to the topsy-turvy world of the Saturnalian festival in ancient Rome, when slaves became kings for a day and were served by their masters. The Feast of Fools, (January 1st.), which appears to have originated in early medieval France also had its roots in this pagan feast and served as a similar outlet for high spirits and fun amongst clergy and the lower classes during the dispiriting days of darkest winter. Mock bishops, popes and priests were often appointed and they frequently wore animal masks, fox-like bishops and porcine popes being particularly popular.

This tradition clearly follows the Roman custom of electing mock kings during the Saturnalia. Inevitably much rowdy and often obscene behaviour ensued. Men dressed up as women and animals, faces were blackened or masked, servants were waited on by their masters. This custom is still continued by our modern armed forces when the ranks are served at table by their officers on Christmas Day. Children became the centre of attention at the Feast of the Juvenalia on January 1st. when they were feted and given freedom of action.

Another aspect of role reversal was manifested by the choice of Boy Bishops on Saint Nicholas Day (December 6th.) until Holy Innocents Day (December 28th.) which was also known as Childermass. It is recorded that their term of office could last for the twenty-two days between these dates, although this was not always the case.

On December 7th 1229, a boy-bishop said vespers before King Edward I who later gave the boy and his companions a generous gift. Saint Nicholas was, according to ancient tradition, a teenage boy when elected to become Bishop of Myra by the elders of the church. This story probably accounts for the rather strange custom of selecting Boy Bishops during the Christmas period. A choir boy was chosen and installed as "bishop" in our medieval churches and cathedrals where he was entitled to celebrate mass and preach sermons. He wore full vestments and carried a pastoral staff. Poor people especially valued his blessing. Boy Bishops were able to appoint their own "canons", "priests" and "deacons". They were usually rewarded with a generous sum of money at the end of their term of office.

In 1481 Rotherham appointed a "Barne (bairn) bishop and it was recorded that,

"A myter be made for the boy-bishop of cloth of gold and with two knopps of silver, gilt and enameled".

Gradually this custom lost its popularity in England and it was eventually banned by Archbishop Cranmer in 1541, although it was briefly revived during the reign of Mary Tudor only to be again forbidden by Elizabeth I.

Our pantomime owes much to these early customs and is a very peculiar mixture of Saturnalian rites, the riotous Lords of Misrule, mummers, masques and commedia dell'arte from Italy which later developed into the Victorian Harlequinade. The word "pantomime" comes from the Latin "pantomimus" which means "playing every role". This dates from the time when just a few actors played many parts by wearing masks to denote their various characters. Mummer's plays were mostly rustic offerings for the local people performed by their neighbours and later the courts developed elaborate and sophisticated masques which had their roots in these ancient revelries. By the reign of Henry VIII Italian style entertainments had been introduced into the English court although the performers were still "disguised" or masked, hence the name "masque".

Edward Hall, writing in 1512, describes just such entertainments at the Court of Henry VIII, one being performed on New Year's Night and the other on Twelfth Night.

"Against New Yeeres night was made in the hall a castell, gates, towers and dungeon, garnished with artillerie and weapon, after the most warlike fashion: and on the front of the castell was written Le fortresse dangereux, and, within the castell were six ladies clothed in russet satin, laid all over with leaves of gold, and everie one knit with laces of blew silke and gold. On their heads,

coifs and caps all of gold. After this castell had been carried about the hall, and the queene had beheld it, in came the king with five other, apparelled in coats, the one halfe of russet sattin, the other halfe of rich cloth of gold; on their heads caps of russet sattin embroidered with works of fine gold bullion.

These six assaulted the castell. The ladies seeing them so lustie and couragious, were content to solace with them, and upon further communication to yeeld the castell, and so they came downe and dansed a long space. And after, the ladies led the knights into the castell, and then the castell suddenly vanished out of their sights. On the daie of the Epiphanie at night, the king, with eleven other, were disguised, after the manner of Italie; called a maske, a thing not seene before, in England; they were aparalled in garments long and broad, wrought all with gold, with visors and caps of gold. And after the banket (banquet) done, these maskers came in with six gentlemen disguised in silke, bearing staffe torches, and desired the ladies to danse; some were content and some refused. And, after they had dansed, and communed together, as the fashion of the maske is, they took their leave and departed, and so did the queene and all the ladies".

It was not the custom for plays or masques to be performed on Christmas Day itself and this annoyed James I who, when told it was not the fashion, replied indignantly that *"I will make it the fashion!"* It is doubtful if he succeeded.

Ben Jonson, Shakespeare's friend and companion, wrote a Masque of Christmas in 1616, which contained many seasonal figures including Father Christmas, who was described as wearing a,

" Doublet and Hose, a High Hat, little Ruffes, white Shoes, his Scarfes and Garters cross tied".

A sophisticated, Malvolio-like figure entirely different from our twentieth century fat, jolly, red-robed Santa. He was accompanied by the characters of Carol and Wassail who were described by Ben Jonson as wearing the following costumes;

"A long tawny coat, with a red cap, and a flute at his girdle, his torch-bearer carrying a song-book open, and Wassail like a neat sempster and songster, her page bearing a brown bowl, drest with ribbands and rosemary before her".

As time went on these courtly masques became more and more elaborate until, by the reign of James I and Charles I, they reached a highly sophisticated form, which was usually based on some classical theme and included music and dance. With the onset of the Civil War and Cromwell's puritanical rule these extravagant courtly entertainments disappeared.

During the eighteenth century theatres sprang up in every town of any size, and theatrical entertainments of every kind were there to be enjoyed by a wide cross section of the public.

Pantomime developed at this time, being a combination of classical story with added song and a Harlequinade, in which dancers mimed the story of lovelorn Harlequin and Columbine. Gradually the other characters such as Scaramouche, Pantaloon and the clown were added. The origin of this Harlequinade was the Italian *commedia dell' arte* which became extremely fashionable as an entertainment in Georgian times along with Italian opera, which was also to be seen on the English stage for the first time. Harlequinades formed an important interlude in Victorian pantomimes and did not entirely disappear until after the First World War.

Fairy stories gradually replaced classical themes, and again role reversal is much in evidence with dames being played by men and principal boys who are really girls!

John Rich was one of the first producers of pantomime in this country, with a production of "The Harlequin Sorcerer" at Lincoln's Inn Field Theatre in 1717. Rich also developed the idea of transformation scenes which were to become an essential part of any Victorian pantomime. The effects were often breathtaking and, on occasions, hilarious. Not everyone, however, enjoyed these extraordinary extravaganzas. In 1867 John Ruskin wrote:

"The Pantomime was, as I said, 'Ali Baba and the Forty Thieves'. The forty thieves were girls. The forty thieves had forty companions who were girls. The forty thieves and their forty companions were in some way mixed up with about four hundred and forty fairies, who were girls. There was an Oxford and Cambridge boat-race, in which the Oxford and Cambridge men were girls. There was a transformation scene, with a forest, in which the flowers were girls, and a chandelier, in which the lamps were girls, and a great rainbow which was all of girls..... Presently after this, came on the forty thieves who, as I told you, were girls; and, there being no thieving to be presently done, and time hanging heavy on their hands, arms and legs, the forty thief-girls proceeded to light forty cigars. Whereupon the British public gave them a round of applause. Whereupon I fell a-thinking; and saw little more of the piece, except as an ugly and disturbing dream."

Joseph Grimaldi, (1779 – 1837) the famous clown and comedian, was one of the Victorian pantomime's best known performers. His hilarious antics led to the introduction of more and more comedy; also the influence of music halls became apparent so that the comedian's spot became an important part of modern pantomime even if it had little relevance to the story. A present day clown is often called "Joey" after this famous nineteenth century comical actor.

"Grimaldi …..the genuine droll, the grimacing, filching, irresistible clown, who laboured so hard in bringing laughter to London that he died prematurely, worn out by his exertions".

In the twentieth century, plays that told a straight-forward story, which could be enjoyed by children, were introduced. Probably the most famous of these is Peter Pan, but others such as, Where The Rainbow Ends, The Bluebird, The Snowman and many more recent productions prove popular with youthful audiences. Boxing Day is the traditional time for Christmas productions to open but this is not always the case with modern shows.

    Pantomime has moved a long way from Saturnalian celebrations and rustic mummers; it has gradually evolved down the centuries until it takes the present day pattern with which we are all familiar. No doubt it will continue to develop and evolve as time passes but essentially it will remain a topsy-turvy world of make-believe and fantasy.

Pantomime

Full of colour song and mirth,
Gives the New Year a happy birth
Costumes beautiful, music bright
A fairy's love, a witch's spite.

Scenes so merry, scenes so sad,
The dames so funny she seems quite mad.
The principal girl so rare and beautiful
Sings away to a lover dutiful.

And so the show ends a happy evening
We are sad to go and still are grieving.
But then, next year it comes again
Despite the weather, hail, snow or rain.

Monica Timmins

18

GAMES

Snap Dragon

Here he comes with flaming bowl,
Don't be mean to take his toll,
Snip! Snap! Dragon!

Take care you don't take too much,
Be not greedy in your clutch,
Snip! Snap! Dragon!

With his blue and lapping tongue
Many of you will be stung,
Snip! Snap! Dragon!

But Old Christmas makes him come
Though he looks so fee! fa! fum!
Snip! Snap! Dragon!

Don't 'ee fear him, be but bold -
Out he goes, his flames are cold,
Snip! Snap! Dragon!   Anon

In earlier, less sophisticated times, people provided their own amusements during the Christmastide celebrations. Families in those days were large, and of course extra guests were often invited to this one big family gathering of the year. After church had been attended, a good Christmas dinner was eaten, well washed down with ale or wine, and the company was then ready to enjoy itself with familiar and sometimes rowdy games, often interspersed with dancing to the strains of a local fiddler. The games were old favourites having been passed on by former generations, and it is interesting to observe many of these perennials still being played at modern Christmas family gatherings: it is probably the only time of year at which they are still enjoyed. People of past and present society have also enjoyed card games and board games over the Yuletide celebrations.

Games were frowned upon by the authorities during past ages. No doubt the sight of poorer people actually enjoying themselves was too much for the ruling classes of the day, and therefore games and gambling of any kind were banned at any time of year excepting Christmas.

Henry VIII issued the following proclamation in the sixteenth century forbidding any:

"Artificer, or craftsman of any handicraft or occupation, Husbandman, Apprentice, Labourer, Servant at husbandry, Journeymen, Servant of the Artificer, Mariner, Fisherman, Waterman or any serving-man to play at Tables, tennis, Dice, Cards, Bowls, Clash, Coyting, Logating, or any other unlawful game, out of Christmas, under pain of twenty shilling to be forfeit for every time; and in Christmas to play at any of the said Games in their Master's houses, or in their Master's presence."

In 1592 three working men were prosecuted for playing bowls in July, *"it being outside the season called Christmas"*, and a few years later in 1613 a man was fined for playing cards on January 10th., just after the Twelve Days of the Christmas period.

No doubt the games were a distraction to many servants and probably they were occasionally responsible for the neglect of their duties, but human nature being what it is, this law seems to have been observed more by its omission rather than its observance, and gambling and games continued to be enjoyed in secret and with discretion at all times of the year.

Many of the games played are of very ancient origin. *"Blindman's Buff"*, or *"Hoodman Blind"*, as it is sometimes known, dates right back far into distant time. Some folklorists believe that this game was the original way in which victims for sacrifice were selected by a blindfolded priest. Certainly there is something quite sinister and scarey in this game which both delights and frightens small children. Their shrieks of joy and apprehension are as loud now as they were five or even ten centuries ago.

"Hot Cockles" was another favourite game, and there are depictions of what appears to be this particular pastime on the wall paintings of Egyptian tombs. It is played in the following way.

One person is blindfolded and ushered into a circle of seated players; the blindfolded person is knelt down in front of one person and places his or her head in their lap (usually it was a man) one of his arms was placed behind or to the side of him, palm uppermost, whilst he shouted *"Hot Cockles. Hot!"*. One person in the room then hit his hand with a stinging blow by means of a rolled up newspaper, slipper or some similar object. The victim then had to identify the person who had hit him. If he guessed correctly, that person took his place or paid a forfeit. Many an old score was probably settled in this game, and often it became rougher and more painful than many people intended.

"Consequences" was another game much enjoyed at parties. Small strips of paper were handed around a circle of players. Each participant then wrote down a man's name, folded the paper

over and then passed it on to his neighbour. Next a woman's name was added and passed on, then a place of meeting, what he said, what she said, and finally the consequence of the tale. The resultant efforts were then read out. Mostly they were banal and rather boring, but in a witty group the results could be both pithy and hilarious. Many people will recall playing this game during birthday and Christmas parties in the days of their youth and it is a game which still emerges from time to time.

"Hunt the Thimble" is another favourite old game, and children find this especially exciting if there is a small prize for the successful finder of the hidden thimble.

"Snap Dragon" was much favoured by our ancestors during the Yuletide festivities. The *"dragon"* was a bowl of flaming brandy into which large raisins had been dropped. The idea was for partygoers to pluck out as many raisins from the flaming *"dragon's mouth"* or bowl as they could. Many a burnt finger must have been sucked afterwards by the children who approached the bowl with both apprehension, excitement, and also shrieks of pain and pleasure. Not a game for the timorous!

"Postman's Knock", was a favourite with the youthful players particularly those of an amorous disposition who looked forward to the resulting kisses, which were not easily obtained in other circumstances, especially in the rather prim society of Victorian England. The game was played in the following way; each girl drew a number out of a hat or bag, they then retired behind a closed door. The "postman" then knocked on the door saying he had a certain amount of "letters" for number so-and-so. Out came the appropriate girl to receive her "letters" (kisses) or not as the case may be, perhaps some young ladies preferred to return their "post" to sender depending upon the attractiveness of the "postman"! In it's time this game was held to be very daring and naughty. The modern liberally minded younger generation would probably find it rather tame when kisses now seem to be there for the asking.

"Musical Chairs" still provides lively entertainment for active partygoers.

"Hide and Seek" was another popular pastime, especially in the large houses which gave plenty of scope for hiding places. Things could, however, go horribly wrong, and the poem, "The Mistletoe Bough", relates a tragic happening said to have been based on an actual occurrence when the hiding place proved to be too good.

> The mistletoe hung in the castle hall,
> The holly branch shone on the old oak wall;
> And the baron's retainers were blithe and gay,
> And keeping their Christmas holiday.
> The baron beheld with a father's pride
> His beautiful child, young Lovell's bride;
> While she with her bright eyes seem'd to be
> The star of the goodly company.
>
> 'I'm weary of dancing now;' she cried;
> 'Here tarry a moment – I'll hide – I'll hide!
> And, Lovell, be sure thou'rt first to trace
> The clue to my secret lurking place.'
> Away she ran – and her friends began
> Each tower to search, and each nook to scan;
> And young Lovell cried, 'Oh where dost thou hide?
> I'm lonesome without thee, my own dear bride.'
>
> They sought her that night! And they sought her next day!
> And they sought her in vain when a week pass'd away!
> In the highest – and lowest – the loneliest spot,
> Young Lovell sought wildly – but found her not.
> And years flew by, and their grief at last
> Was told as a sorrowful tale long past;
> And when Lovell appeared, the children cried,
> 'See! The old man weeps for his fairy bride.'

At length an oak chest, that had long lain hid,
Was found in the castle – they raised the lid –
And a skeleton form lay mouldering there,
In the bridal wreath of that lady fair!
Oh! sad was her fate! – in sportive jest
She hid from her lord in the old oak chest.
It closed with a spring! – and, dreadful doom,
The bride lay clasp'd in her living tomb!

Thomas Haynes Bayly (1797-1839)

"Forfeits" was a popular game with young and old in the past and was played by ordinary people in their homes, but it was also enjoyed at the courts of various kings and queens including Charles II and his courtiers. It is played in the following fashion;

Some personal possession, such as a ribbon, shoe, tie or piece of jewellery is collected from every player. These are then placed all together in a sack or box and the participants must then regain their belongings by performing a forfeit.

An item at random is held up by a blindfolded player who says, *"Here is a thing and a very pretty thing, what will the owner of this pretty thing do?"*. A suitable task or forfeit is thought up such as standing on their heads, singing a song, or, most dreaded of all by small boys and looked forward to by older ones, kissing all the girls in the room. The players are not allowed to regain their belongings until the task is successfully accomplished. If this is the case, they then change places with the blindfolded person and hold out the next object and name the task in the appropriate manner.

A Game of Forfeits with the Blushing Fair

Or, if to *forfeits* they the sport confine,
The happy folk, adjacent to the fire,
Their stations take; excepting one alone
(Sometimes the social Mistress of the house)
Who sits within the centre of the room,

To cry the *pawns*: much is the laughter, now,
Arising solely from the awkward lot
As such as can't the *Christmas catch* repeat,
And who, perchance, are sentenc'd to salute
The jetty beauties of the *chimney-back,*
Or *lady's shoe;* others, more lucky far,
By hap, or favor, meet a sweeter doom,
And, on each fair-one's lovely lips imprint
The ardent *kiss;* blushing, the maiden, coy,
With fruitless strength, endeavours to resist
The am'rous youth, and shun his warm embrace;
Whilst fir'd with transport, he pursues the bliss,
Nor rests until the pleasing task's complete.

Romaine Joseph Thorn.
Christmas, a Poem. (1795)

Mr Fezziwig's jolly Christmas ball from illustrations by
John Leech (1817-1864), for Charles Dicken's,
"A Christmas Carol"

Note the kissing bough hanging from the ceiling.

19

WASSAIL

Wassail, wassail all over town!
Our toast it is white, and our ale it is brown,
Our bowl it is made of the white maple tree;
With the wassailing bowl we'll drink to thee.

So here is to Cherry and to his right cheek,
Pray God send our master a good piece of beef,
And a good piece of beef that may we all see;
With the wassailing bowl we'll drink to thee.

Come, butler, come fill us a bowl of the best,
Then we hope that your soul in heaven may rest;
But if you do draw us a bowl of the small,
Then down shall go butler, bowl and all.

Then here's to the maid in the lily white smock,
Who tripped to the door and slipped back the lock!
Who tripped to the door and pulled back the pin
For to let these jolly wassailers in.

(Part of the Gloucestershire Wassail Song which was sung to Ralph Vaughan Williams, by an old man of that county)

The word "wassail" comes from the Anglo Saxon WAS HAEL, which meant be whole, be healthy, or "good health", as we still say when we drink to one another.

Wassail bowls were often made of polished wood; "our bowl is made of the good maplin tree", goes one carol; another "our bowl it is of the white maple tree" and yet another variation runs: "the cup it is made of the good ashen tree". Lignum - Vitae, a wood which is hard as iron and impervious to liquids, was made into the more expensive bowls and often the rims were bound in silver.

They were decorated with evergreens and ribbons and filled with mulled, spiced wine, cider or ale. This was taken from house to house, to the accompaniment of wassail carols. Householders drank a little of the mixture, topped up the bowl and gave alms to the wassailers - a welcome addition to poor people's pockets during the Christmas season.

Often "lambswool" or "lamsagel" was the mixture placed in the bowl. A seventeenth century recipe goes as follows:

"Boil three pints of ale, beat six eggs, the whites and yolks together; set both to the fire in a pewter pot; add roasted apples, sugar, beaten nutmegs, cloves and ginger and, being well brewed, drink it while hot."

The "roasted crabs hissing in the bowl" referred to by Shakespeare in his poem Winter, are roasted crab apples spluttering in the mulled ale and not the crabs found in the sea.

In the West Country and the Midlands it was the custom to Wassail the apple trees during the Christmas season, but more often the ceremony took place during the New Year and right up to January 16th.(which was the eve of Twelfth Night by the old calendar). The ceremony undoubtedly originates from the ancient tree worshipping ceremonies of our ancestors.

The apple tree was venerated because of its connection with mistletoe (like the oak with its oak *"apples"*). The tree in the Garden of Eden was traditionally an apple tree, although it is not stated as being so in the Bible. Both the Romans and the Celts held apple trees to be sacred and imposed penalties on those who cut them down.

Avalon, the kingdom of the dead in Celtic mythology, means the Green Apple Island, where mystic apples grew which promoted healing. According to Arthurian legend, it was to this island that King Arthur was ferried on a barge by the queens after being mortally wounded in battle.

Votive offerings were given to apple trees in order to please the tree spirits and to promote a good harvest. This has come down to us in the Wassailing Ceremony which still takes place in the West Country. A bowl containing hot spiced cider with pieces of toast on the top is taken into the orchard. Each man present drinks a little of the mixture in a cup and throws the rest of the liquid into the trees' roots as a libation to the god of tree fertility. A piece of the soaked toast is placed in the crook of a branch and sometimes salt as well *"for robin"* who represents the tree spirit. Shotguns are then fired into the branches to discourage evil spirits and awaken the tree for the oncoming spring. It is encouraged to produce a good crop by the following verse (although there are many local variations):

> *Apple tree, apple tree, I wassail thee*
> *To blow and to bear*
> *Hat vulls, cap vulls, dree bushel bag vulls,*
> *And my pockets vull too, hip, hip, hurrah.*

In days gone by the women would have been busy in the farm kitchen preparing a hot supper whilst this ceremony took place. Afterwards the men knocked at the door but they were not allowed in until they could guess which particular meat was being cooked that night - no doubt the delicious smell gave it away.

Cider was very much the drink enjoyed by the farming people in days gone by and so it was most important to encourage the trees to bear a good crop. Most farms and country houses produced their own supplies of cider which, with luck, would last them throughout the coming year. This was a most potent drink with a high alcohol content. Thomas Hardy writes about the over indulgence of farm workers during a Harvest Supper in his book, "Far from the Madding Crowd", and relates the tragic events which followed due to their drunkenness, during a destructive storm which threatened the precious hayricks. Ale was also home brewed on many farms and manors. It was far safer to drink cider or ale than water, which in past ages was often impure or polluted. Wine was a great luxury which poor people rarely drank. Cider and ale, usually mulled and spiced, provided them with their share of Christmas cheer.

A Somerset wassail bowl

20

NEW YEAR'S EVE - HOGMANAY

The log was burning brightly
'Twas a night that should banish all sin,
For the bells were ringing the Old Year out,
And the New Year in.

The Miner's Dream of Home.
William Godwin.(1756-1836)

We wish you a merry Christmas, a happy New Year
A pocket full of money and a cellar full of beer,
A good fat pig to last you all the year
Please to give us a New Year's Gift to cheer.

Old Welsh rhyme

Medieval England celebrated New Year on March 25th (Lady Day) and in many instances it remains the date for the financial new year in commerce. This was largely due to the influence of the church, who wished to replace the pagan New Year with one dedicated to Our Lady. The date of March 25th also coincided with the arrival of springtime and new growth bursting from the ground; it was truly indicative of a new beginning for the agricultural year and maybe the church also had this in mind when choosing March 25th as the date. It was never wholly accepted by the people and a confusing state of affairs existed for centuries until the change over to the Gregorian calendar in 1752 when January 1st was once again made the official New Year's Day with Lady Day remaining a Quarter Day, when rents and debts became due.

In Roman times the feast of the Kalends took place in January and it was at these festivities that the STRENAE, or gifts, were distributed to relatives, friends and servants. January derives its name from the two-faced god JANUS; with one face he looked back into the old year and with the other he looked forward and outward into the New Year. The figure of Old Father Time with his scythe probably originates from this figure of Janus with overtones of Odin thrown in for good measure; he too roamed the world at this time of year according to Norse mythology.

New Year has never been quite as popular in England as Christmas, and until the Reformation, Christmas was also Scotland's chief festival. At that time the stern Presbyterian Church of Scotland decided to do away with such pagan Yuletide festivities during the religious celebration of Christ's birth and so the people transferred their festive attentions to New Year which is ironic, since the festivities developed into an extremely rowdy and purely secular holiday - more heathen by far than the old Christmas festival which did, at least, retain some semblance of godly religious observance.

Gradually the festivities became known as Hogmanay to all people north of the border. There are several theories as to how this name originated: one is that it comes from the Anglo-Saxon words HALEG MONATH, which mean THE HOLY MONTH. Another explanation is that the Gaelic words OGE MAIDNE (new morning) are the original source; and yet another school of thought inclines to the theory that the French HOGUINANA (lead to the mistletoe) came across to Scotland during the years of "The Auld Alliance"; at one time first-footers always carried a piece of mistletoe and greenery on their New Year's Eve perambulations. Probably we will never know for sure how the word arrived into our language.

New Year is the time of new beginnings, a time to start afresh and discard all that is stale and shoddy. In consequence people believed that it was necessary to begin the New Year clear of all debt, with a clean house shining from attic to cellar; all linen was washed and everyone used to put on clean clothes, bed-linen was changed on New Year's Eve so that the bed was fresh for New Year's Day.

It was deemed unlucky to wash clothes on New Year's Day itself. An old rhyme says:

"Wash on New Year's Day
Wash one of the family away".

It was also thought unlucky to receive new shoes on New Year's Day.

It was felt necessary to have money in your pocket, food in your larder, and fuel for your fire at this time in order to set a pattern of plenty for the months to come.

Just before midnight on New Year's Eve as much noise as possible was made; bells were rung, pots and pans were beaten, guns were fired, people shouted and sang in order to frighten away any evil spirits and discourage them from entering the imminently close New Year. It was a lot of fun, too!

In some areas all doors and windows were opened in a house to "let out" the Old Year, together with any ill luck or sorrow which still lurked in the shadows. After midnight had struck, the doors and windows were tightly shut so that the home could be fumigated by means of a smouldering Juniper branch which purified the building and its inhabitants, as well as driving out disease.

First Footing is probably the most famous custom connected with HOGMANAY. The man who first foots (it is disastrous for a woman to do so!) must be dark, sound in wind and limb and without blemish; in certain parts of Scotland it is preferable for a red-headed man to perform the ceremony.

On the whole, blond men are not in demand and it is thought that this dates from Viking times when a tall, blond, able-bodied man suddenly arriving at your door could mean death and disaster to the householder. If, however, an undesirable person such as a cripple, a blond or, dread the thought, a woman, accidentally let in the New Year the event could be rectified by means of throwing salt on the fire, or by placing a burning coal in a bowl of water as these were ancient acts of purification.

The First Footer should carry gifts of coal, salt and bread, or coal, bread and a bottle of whisky. This signified an abundance of food, warmth and good cheer during the coming year.

The first footer would enter by the front door, thus letting the New Year in, and leave by the back door chasing the old one out. Before he left, a "wee dram" was enjoyed by all present, together with "black bun" which was a rich, dark plum cake, similar to our Christmas cake, but instead of being iced it was encased in pastry. Some Scots still make and eat this delicious confection, but it is not so widely enjoyed as in former times.

Sowens were drunk in the north of Scotland; this was a sort of thin porridge or gruel to which honey and whisky was added. Sometimes bowls of it were taken from house to house when first-footing. A little was smeared on the door-posts before the householders sampled the delicious brew.

By the time First Footers had enjoyed hospitality at several households in return for "letting in" the New Year, they probably emerged much less sure footed as the night, or rather the morning, progressed.

Sometimes songs were sung by groups of First Footers doing the rounds and going from door to door. The following words are part of a song noted down in Orkney:

> *We houp your ale is stark and stout,*
> *For men to drink the auld year out.*
> *Ye ken the weather's snow and sleet,*

Stir up the fire to warm our feet.
Our shoon's made o' mare's skin,
Come open the door and let us in.

It was essential for a fire to be kept blazing in the hearth throughout New Year's Eve and on into New Year's Day until its close at midnight; this ensured a warm and welcoming home during the year to come.

Fire festivals of various kinds take place throughout the northern counties of England, and Scotland during the early weeks of the year. Allendale has its blazing tar barrels; Burghead, Morayshire, burns the Clavie on January 11th, the equivalent of old New Year's Eve (Clavie is a Gaelic word meaning basket, as in fire-basket); Swinging the Fireballs takes place at Stonehaven, Kincardineshire, on New Year's Eve to burn the Old Year out (the fireballs are made from old rags soaked in paraffin, encased in chicken wire-netting, and suspended from a length of wire; these are swung around the celebrants' heads); Up-Helly-Aa, a Norse fire-festival, is celebrated at Lerwick, Shetland. on the last Tuesday in January, when a replica Viking ship is set ablaze; afterwards the Jarl and his guizers walk the island, dancing, singing and drinking until dawn. The words "Up-Helly-Aa" mean "the ending of the holy-days". All these fire festivals signify the driving out of the evil by means of the sacred element of purifying fire.

Wales used to have many New Year customs but they have largely died out. Two of the most charming are the CALENNIG and PERILLANS which used to be paraded through the streets of towns and villages by Welsh children. The CALENNIG consists of an apple stuck all over with ears of corn which is mounted on a tripod of sticks and crowned with a sprig of holly. These strange objects (presumably symbolising fertility and plenty) were taken around whilst appropriate carols were sung by children who received alms in return for their efforts. The PERILLAN was a semi-circular wooden tray surrounded by a lip which confined an arrangement of different greenery; this was taken from house to house at New Year and alms and gifts were given as a reward to the young people participating.

A calennig

A perillan.

The extraordinary and somewhat macabre MARI LWYD (grey mare), or Y GYNFASFARCH (the canvas horse) is taken around the houses between December 24th – January 6th in South Wales, and in particular at Maesteg, Glamorgan. It is accompanied by a

Mare-leader, a Sergeant, and a Merryman (fiddler), together with Punch and Judy; also Morris dancers sometimes join the company. A knock is made on the door and ritualistic questions ensue, such as:

>Wel, dyma ni'n dwad
>Gyfeillion diniwad
>I mofyn am gennad i ganu.

(Here we come, simple friends to ask permission to sing.)

The householders reply:
>Rhowch glywed, wyr doethion
>Pa faint ych o ddynion
>A pheth yn wych union yw'ch enwau.

(Let us hear, oh! wise men, how many you are, and what are your names?)

After many such questions and answers the Mari Lwyd enters the house snapping at the company and chasing them around the room. A carol is sung and good wishes for the New Year are exchanged. The head of this amazing creature is made from a horse's skull (sometimes carved wood) and the jaws are made to snap by a man under white sheeting which comprises the "horse's" body. Much teasing takes place and of course children loved being scared by this monster. It is interesting that many of these New Year ceremonies take place in the Celtic fringes of our country.

Another strange custom was called "Drawing the Cream": this entailed drawing water from the well or stream as soon as possible on New Year's Day usually during the early hours of the morning. This first bucket of water was called the "cream", or sometimes the "flower", and it foretold an early marriage to the drawer if single, and children to a married woman. Women vied with each other to obtain this very first bucketful of new magical water. Often children went around with New Year water and splashed anyone they met as a blessing; sometimes they were allowed to sprinkle people with the new water as they lay in bed which is obviously an old symbol of fecundity. The following is one of the songs sung on this occasion:

> *Here we bring new water*
> *From the well so clear,*
> *For to worship God with*
> *This happy New Year.*
> *Sing levy dew, sing levy dew,*
> *The water and the wine;*
> *The seven bright gold wires*
> *And bugles they do shine.*
>
> *Sing reign of Fair Maid,*
> *With gold upon her toe-*
> *Open you the West Door,*
> *And tell the Old Year go:*
> *Sing reign the Fair Maid,*
> *With gold upon her chin-*
> *Open you the East Door*
> *And let the New Year in.*

It has been suggested that the "Fair Maid" could originally have been Aurora (EOS), the pagan goddess of the dawn who was later, in Christian times gradually transformed into the figure of the Virgin Mary; the strange phrase "levy dew" could have originally been "levez Dieu" (God has risen). The west door is obviously sunset and the east door dawn. The words "golden" and "shining" could indicate the dawning of a propitious new year, but what did the seven golden wires and the shining bugles signify? It is evident that the verse is to do with water and the New Year, but its original ancient meaning has been lost through time.

In Scotland the peculiar practice of SAINING took place on New

Year's Day. On the previous evening human urine was collected and kept until the following day; this was called Magic Water, probably due to its high alcoholic content. This was sprinkled on every wall, door, and inhabitant of the house as a form of blessing. It is difficult to say how this custom arose or the significance of the original ceremony.

Coventry Godcakes were special to that city, being given by godparents to their godchildren, who visited them on New Year's Day to receive their blessing. This custom continued until at least the 1930s, but has now disappeared. The godcakes were triangular in shape symbolizing the Trinity interestingly, the parish church of the city is called after the Holy Trinity, and so this custom could date back to its medieval foundation. The cakes are similar to Eccles Cakes, but have a flaky pastry casing. The recipe is as follows:

Coventry Godcakes

The filling:
- 4 ozs currants
- 1 oz finely chopped candied peel
- ½ teaspoon of both allspice and nutmeg
- 2 oz caster sugar, 1 oz butter.

Flaky or puff pastry

1). Put all the ingredients into a pan and heat for a few minutes, then turn into a basin to cool.
2). Roll out the pastry to about 1/4 inch thickness. Cut into 7 inch squares, and place a good tablespoon of the cooled mixture on one side of the square; fold over the opposite side to form a triangle. Pinch the edges together and fold neatly under.
3). Flatten the cakes gently with a rolling pin and then slash the tops several times with a sharp knife. Place on a greased baking sheet and bake for 10 to 15 minutes in a hot oven. When cooked sprinkle with caster sugar and leave to cool.

Coventry Godcakes

This rather charming custom must have created a special bond between godparents and their charges in the past.

The making of New Year resolutions continues although most people fail miserably in their well-meant endeavours. On January 2nd 1664 Samuel Pepys recorded the following resolution in his diary:

"I came to a new vowe, that I will not see above one play in a month at any publique theatres till the sum of 50s. be spent and then none before New Year's Day unless I do become worth £1,000 sooner than then. So to the King's House and I saw 'The Usurper' which is no good play, though better than that what I saw yesterday..."

Pepys loved the theatre and he found his resolution wavering in spite of his impecunious state. However, by the following year he appears to have improved his monetary position, for he writes on New Year's Eve 1664:

"After dinner to my accounts of the whole yeare, and was at it till twelve at night, it being bitter cold. But yet I was well satisfied with my worke, and above all to find myself, by the great blessing of God, worth £1,349..........Thence home to eat a little,

and so to bed. Soon as ever the clock struck one I kissed my wife in the kitchen by the fireside, wishing her a merry New Yeare, observing that I was the first proper wisher of it this year, for I did it as soon as ever the clock struck one."

He does not appear to have spent his New Year's Eves in a boisterous manner on most occasions; instead, he reckoned up his accounts for the year hoping he would be soundly in credit.

England does not, on the whole, celebrate New Year with the verve and enthusiasm of our northern cousins. Christmas is, for most people, the family festival, and New Year belongs more to friends and social gatherings. Young and old, however, still use the occasion as an excuse for high spirited behaviour, parties, and the annual vigil of seeing in the New Year frequently encourages scenes of wild and drunken pranks. This is no new pattern of behaviour, for even in Roman times the more sober-minded citizens recorded their disapproval of riotous Saturnalian gatherings.

A Frenchman, Louis Simon, wrote the following account of Hogmanay celebrations in Edinburgh 1811:

"There is no sleeping the first night of the year in Edinburgh. About midnight it is a received custom for the common people to give a kiss to any woman in the streets, on foot or in carriages. Few women expose themselves to this rude salutation. But the streets are full, notwithstanding, of unruly boys who knock on house doors, and make noise all night. This is a little relic of the coarse manners of former times, which is still tolerated."

New Year is the time for divination and the foretelling of our futures; once this was done by ritualistic means but now we study our stars and the astrologers' yearly predictions in the daily newspapers - a different method but the end result is much the same.

A great deal of weather lore exists for this time of year and an old rhyme states:

> If New Year's Eve night wind blow south
> That betokeneth warmth and growth
> If west, much milk and fish in the sea
> If north, much cold and storms will be
> If east, the trees will bear much fruit
> If north-east - flee it man and brute.

Unmarried girls would attempt to look into their futures and ascertain if a husband was to be found. One method was to tie nine holly leaves into a handkerchief tied with nine knots; this would be placed under their pillow in the hope that they would dream of their future spouse, though it is probable a nightmare was the more likely outcome with such an uncomfortable object as a bedfellow.

Another method was to drop melted candle-wax into a bowl of cold water at the stroke of midnight on New Year's Eve in the hope that the resulting shape would form the initial of the future husband's name. These rustic style oracles may seem to be superstitious nonsense to us, but it must be remembered that in the past it was essential for a woman to find a husband in order to ensure economic security and an accepted place in society. Most women were unable to become economically independent unless they inherited wealth on their husband's death, and spinsters were looked down on, often being only barely tolerated by more fortunate relatives. Any sign of marriage was welcomed.

New Year is a time of sadness and gladness, of regrets and optimism, of looking back to what has passed and forwards to what will be. The old god Janus is still king of this particular festival.

The New Year

I am the little New Year, ho, ho!
Here I come tripping it over the snow,
Shaking my bells with a merry din
So open your doors and let me in!

Presents I bring for each and all,
Big folks, little folks, short and tall;
Each one from me a treasure may win
So open your doors and let me in!

Some shall have silver and some shall have gold,
Some shall have new clothes and some shall have old;
Some shall have brass and some shall have tin,
So open yours doors and let me in!

Some shall have water and some shall have milk,
Some shall have satin and some shall have silk,
But each from me a present may win
So open your doors and let me in!

Traditional

21

THE ABOLITION of CHRISTMAS

"Dost thou think that because thou art virtuous there shall be no more cakes and ale?"

Sir Toby Belch.
Twelfth Night.   W.Shakespeare

"Old Christmas now is come to town though few do him regard."

Mercurius Democritus. 1652

The coming of the Reformation in 1517 created an upsurge of Protestant feeling and this took on an austere and puritanical form amongst certain sections of the community. The Puritans became a very vocal minority denouncing anything remotely popish or even enjoyable.

By Elizabeth I reign, Puritans were already denouncing Lords of Misrule, gluttony and eventually all Christmas traditions and

The Vindication of
CHRISTMAS

IN the name of the King of Kings, and Prince of peace; in imitation of my great and glorious Lord and Master Jesus Christ, and in love to them that hate me, I am come to them that love me not. And as my good Master did know how courſly he ſhould be dealt withall (by misbelieving hard-hearted Jews) yet he came on this day from whom I have my name of *Christmas*, or Chriſts Day: Even ſo, when I come this 25 of December, though I know I ſhall be hard-

> Keep out, you come not here,

> Sir, I bring good cheere.

> Old Chriſtmas welcome; Do not fear.

22 Imprinted at London for G. Horton, 1653.

An anonymous seventeenth century pamphlet

celebrations. The Presbyterian Church in Scotland had banned the celebration of Christmas as early as 1583, and although Charles I attempted to revive it in 1618, the General Assembly re-imposed the ban. Even today Christmas, although reinstated as a Scottish public holiday, remains very much a second rate festival when compared to Hogmanay (New Year's Eve). The Scottish church leaders even forbade snowballing and football as well as the more usual social activities of dancing, singing and gambling.

During the reign of James I Christmas entertainments became more extravagant and frequently the masques presented had pagan themes which were abhorrent to the Puritans.

At first they only objected to the excesses of Christmas, such as dancing, gambling, over-indulgence in food and drink but later, they sought to reform the season. As time passed their attitude became more and more narrow-minded and bigoted although, it must be said, that rowdy and excessive behaviour was apparent during the Yuletide festivities owing more to the pagan gods than the Christian one.

Philip Stubbes wrote the following words in his "Anatomie of Abuses" (1583):

"But the true celebration of the Feast of Christmas is to meditat (and as it were to ruminat) uppon the incarnation and byrthe of Jesus Christ, not onely that time, but all the tymes and daies of our life, and to shew our selves thankeful to his Maiestie for the same. Notwithstanding, who is ignorant that more mischiefe is that time committed than in all the yeere besides? What masking and mumming! whereby robberie, whoredom, murther, and what not is committed. What dicing and carding, what eating and drinking, what banqueting and feasting is then used more than in all the yeere besydes! to the great dishonour of GOD and the impoverishing of the realm."

It is clear that to many sober minded Christians religious observance seemed to take a secondary place in the Christmas celebrations; a state of affairs which remains apparent today. A puzzled William Prynne asked:

"Why could not the English nation observe festivals and especially Christmas without drinking, roaring, healthing, dicing, carding, masques and stage plays? which better become the sacrifices of Bacchus, than the resurrection, the incarnation of our most blessed Saviour....Heathens and infidels would", he went on, *"Think our Saviour to be a glutton, an epicure, a wine-bibber, a devil, a friend of publicans and sinners....CHRIST-MASSE may more truly be stiled DIVELS-MASSE OR SATURNES-MASSE..."*

Histrio-Mastix (1633)

By the time of the Civil War the Puritans views became more vocal and with the defeat and the execution of Charles I in 1649 they, at last, were able to subdue all worldly aspects of the Christmas Feast.

In 1652 an Act of Parliament was passed which forbade the celebration of Christmas. It read as follows:

"No observation shall be had of the five and twentieth day of December, commonly called Christmas Day; nor any solemnity used or exercised in churches upon that day in respect thereof."

For some time before the official Act of Parliament was passed, many authorities had banned Christmas festivities in their own particular areas. In London, 1647, the authorities attempted to enforce local legislation which stated that: *"All festivals or holidays heretofore superstitiously used were no longer to be observed"*. All shops and places of business were to remain open and no special services were to be held in the churches. Of course, many people were unhappy about this state of affairs and acted in defiance. Riots took place all over the country. At Ipswich several people were killed whilst demonstrating; in Canterbury the Mayor, who had tried to insist on the opening of the market and shops, was knocked down; and in Oxford, a Royalist stronghold, many citizens were injured. With the passing of the Act, Christmas was driven underground for eight years until the restoration of Charles II in 1660. Of course, people continued to observe Christmas in the privacy of their own homes and services were still held in defiance of the authorities, although they risked fines and imprisonment if caught doing so. Country areas were able to escape close vigilance by the authorities, but larger towns, and especially London, were under close scrutiny and faced penalties if found transgressing the law regarding Christmas and other festivals.

The diarist John Evelyn reports the sad state of affairs which existed at this time in his diary:

"25th Dec.,1652 Christmas-day, no sermon any where, no church being permitted to open, so observed it at home. The next day, we went to Lewisham, where an honest divine preached.

25th Dec.,1654 Christmas-day. No public offices in churches, but penalties on observers, so I was constrained to celebrate it at home.

25th Dec.,1655. There was no more notice taken of Christmas-day in churches."

These prohibitions do not appear to have quelled his spirits or his determination to celebrate Christmas Day in time honoured fashion, for two years later he wrote:

"25th Dec., 1657 I went to London with my wife, to celebrate Christmas-day, Mr Gunning preaching in Exeter chapel on Micah vii,2. Sermon ended, as he was giving us the Holy Sacrament, the chapel was surrounded with soldiers, and all the communicants and assembly surprised and kept prisoners by them, some in the house, others carried away. It fell to my share to be confined to a room in the house, where yet I was permitted to dine with the master of it, the Countess of Dorset, Lady Hatton, and some others of quality who invited me. In the afternoon came Colonel Whalley, Goffe, and others, from Whitehall to examine us one by one; some they committed to the Marshal, some to prison. When I came before them, they took my name and abode, examined me why, contrary to the ordinance made, that none should any

longer observe the superstitious time of the Nativity (so esteemed by them), I durst offend, and particularly be at Common Prayers, which they told me was but the mass in English, and particularly pray for Charles Stuart; for which we had no scripture. I told them we did not pray for Charles Stuart, but for all Christian Kings, Princes, and Governors. They replied, in so doing we prayed for the King of Spain, too, who was their enemy and a Papist, with other frivolous and ensnaring questions, and much threatening; and, finding no colour to detain me, they dismissed me with much pity of my ignorance. These were men of high flight and above ordinances, and spake spiteful things of our Lord's Nativity. As we went up to receive the Sacrament, the miscreants held their muskets against us, as if they would have shot us at the altar, but yet suffering us to finish the office of Communion, as perhaps not having instructions what to do, in case they found us in that action. So I got home late the next day, blessed be God!"

Not everyone escaped punishment; a Hugh Peters was accused of "preaching against Christmas Day and then eating two mincepies for his dinner!" Lord Fairfax, a leading Parliamentarian, was fined for attending a comedy at Christmas time. Nor were all Protestant clergymen unsympathetic to the old ways. Many had liberal attitudes towards worship and they must have found the restrictions irksome and extreme. George Herbert expressed just such a sensible attitude:

"The country parson is a lover of old customs, if they be good and harmless; and then rather because country people are much addicted to them, so that to favour them therein is to win their hearts, and to oppose them therein is to deject them. If there be any ill in the custom, that may be severed from the good, he pares the apple and gives them the clean to feed on."

A Priest to the Temple. 1632. (Published in 1651)

For every pamphlet or book which was published decrying Christmas another anonymous publication appeared in its defence, including the well-known *"Vindication of Christmas"* published in 1653, in which Father Christmas (who was shown on the cover in contemporary seventeenth century dress) searches for a place in which to keep the traditional Christmas, and eventually finds it alive and well in a Devon farmhouse:

"We discoursed merrily, without either profaneness or obscenity....the hinds and maidservants and ploughboys skipped and leaped for joy, singing a carol to the tune of hey."

When the Pilgrim Fathers and other settlers established their colonies in the New World because of their strict religious beliefs, their views on Christmas observancies were adhered to with religious fervour.

In 1659, the General Court of Massachusetts passed a law which stated:

"Anybody who is found observing, by abstinence from labour, feasting, or in any other way, any such daye as Christmas day, shall pay for every offense five shillings."

Life must have been hard and joyless, without festivals to brighten the days. If anything, the American Puritan sects were even stricter and more rigid in their views than their British counterparts.

William Bradford wrote a journal in 1620 which describes the attitudes held by the American brethren of Plymouth Colony:

"On ye day called Christmas Day, ye Gov'r (Governor) called them out to work (as was used) but ye most of this company excused themselves, and said it went against their consciences to work on ye day. So ye Gov'r tould them that if they made it a matter of conscience, he would spare them until they were better informed. So he led away ye rest, and left them: but when they came home at noone from their worke, he found them in ye streete at play, openly; some pitching ye barr, and some at stoole ball, and such like

sports. So he went to them and took away their implements and told them it was against his conscience that they should play and others worke. If they made ye keeping of it matter of devotion, let them kepe their houses, but there should be no gameing or revelling in ye streets. Since which time nothing hath been attempted that way, at least, openly."

Gradually more and more colonists arrived from Europe bringing with them varying political and religious beliefs; this modified many of the earlier attitudes and the old narrow ways were kept only amongst the strictest sects. The state of Alabama was one of the first to make Christmas Day a public holiday in 1836. Within a few years other states were following suit, Oklahoma being the last one to do so in 1890.

It is ironic that many of the more worldly and commercial aspects of Christmas should have travelled back across the Atlantic to us from the very country that, for years, most abhorred the very idea of Christmas.

In England, the repression of all festivities continued until the death of Oliver Cromwell in 1658 and the break-up of the Commonwealth. With the return of Charles II in 1660 there was an explosion of joy. Social values were once again upended although some of the more extreme customs and rowdy behaviour never returned. Puritan values had moderated our festival of Christmas; however people could again, openly, wish one another a heartfelt "Merry Christmas".

Snap Dragon

Where is *Snap-Dragon?* all extinguished - vanished!
Where mystic *Mistletoe?* unfairly banish'd,
To grace the kitchen, and I live to tell it!
Where's *Blind Man's Buff?* alas! this march of mind,
With all its boasted blessings, hath refined,
Us out of half our former recreations!

Where is old *Hunt the Slipper?* with the snow
Which melted, many, many years ago.
Where *Forfeits,* paid (I hate alterations)
In cunning Cupid's current coinage, kisses?
Despatched to Coventry to Modern misses.

Where are the *'Country Dances'*, once promoted
To such distinction in our revels? Voted
Old fashion'd as the Laird of Batmawhapple.
'Cast off' 'Pousette' the modish belle derides,
As figures rude as Runic ones; *'Change Sides'*
Is practised only in St.Stephen's Chapel.

                        The Humorist.   William Harrison. 1832.

THE
TRYAL
OF
Old Father *Chriſtmas*,

FOR

Encouraging his MAJESTY's Subjects in Idleneſs, Gluttony, Drunkenneſs, Gaming, Swearing, Rioting, and all Manner of Extravagance and Debauchery.

At the Aſſizes held in the

CITY of PROFUSION,

BEFORE

The Lord Chief Juſtice CHURCHMAN, Mr. Juſtice FEAST, Mr. Juſtice GAMBOL, and ſeveral other his Majeſty's Juſtices of Oyer and Terminer and Goal Delivery.

By JOSIAH KING.

LONDON:
Printed and Sold by T. BOREMAN near *Child*'s Coffee-Houſe, in St. *Paul's Church-yard*; and Sold likewiſe at his Shop at the *Cock* on *Ludgate-hill.*
M DCC XXXV.

An eighteenth century broadsheet dated 1735

Epiphany

The Wise Men came,
Not kings
But men of wisdom.
Bringing with them gifts
Of determination, endurance and humility,
Also other more worldly trifles.
They arrived to find
Devious ploys to use their knowledge
And saw straight through the lies.
The Child, they found,
Was not what they expected.
A humble family
With a lamb-like babe.
They pondered long and hard
Coming to the conclusion
That this Child was different
A man who would change the world,
Cast away the old gods,
Lead men to new ways.
But these ways were unforseen
The journey had been prolonged, tedious,
Full of uncertainty and doubt.
Its conclusion was unexpected.
They waited to see what
The future would disclose
And, wisely, kept their
Musings to themselves.

Monica Evans

22

TWELFTH NIGHT, EPIPHANY and CANDLEMAS

"Our revels now are ended."

"The Tempest". William Shakespeare.

There is some confusion as to whether January 5th or January 6th is the Twelfth Day. Many people continue to regard the latter as correct but if we count Christmas Night (December 25th) as the first it follows that January 5th is the twelfth day and night; also January 6th is The Feast of the Epiphany, the church festival which follows Christmas. In spite of this, Twelfth Night and Day celebrations have taken place on January 6th for centuries. It's all very illogical, and probably means that many people who thought they had taken down their decorations on time to avoid ill-luck were, in fact, a day late!

The Twelve Days of Christmas did not comprise a complete period of time free from all work for the poor; essential work on the farm which entailed the feeding of livestock, milking, dairy work, etc., continued, and most shops and businesses only shut on Christmas Day itself. A familiar example of this occurs in "A Christmas Carol" by Charles Dickens, in which he describes the begrudging manner of Scrooge who allows his clerk, Bob Cratchit, to take only Christmas Day off as a holiday, and later on in the story asks a boy in the street if the butcher's shop is still trading even on Christmas morning!

No wonder there were riots when the Puritans tried to take away that precious day's holiday from the populace. Throughout the Twelve Days various festivities took place, though not continuously.

Work on the wet or frozen land was suspended; ploughing, hedging and ditching, manuring the land, etc., had to wait for better conditions and so a little more leisure time was available to landworkers. Until a hundred years ago, Britain was still largely an agrarian society with few rights and even fewer holidays. Annual festivals, such as Mothering Sunday, Easter, and Christmas together with the more secular festivities of May Day and Mid-Summer etc, provided the only enjoyment for most working people and gave release and change from the daily drudgery of work. Christmas was the great holiday of the year and, in consequence, much was made of the final night, with parties and wild festivities being the rule rather than the exception. Twelfth Night celebrations were common right up to late Victorian times, but then seemed to decline, and by the time of the First World War they disappeared completely - even the Twelfth Night Cake became a Christmas Cake!

In 1752 the Gregorian calendar was introduced into Britain as we had become completely out of kilter with the rest of Europe (some ten days difference). They had gone over to this more accurate system of calculation in the sixteenth century as indeed had Scotland. As a result of all this, eleven days were chopped out of the calendar for that year which meant our Christmas Day now fell eleven days earlier than formerly. Old Christmas Eve now fell on January 5th, and Old Christmas Day on the new January 6th. Many country people continued to use the old dates, as the new system made them feel they had been cheated out of eleven days of their lives; this situation must have been extremely confusing. Rioting took place with people chanting *"Give us back our eleven days!"* To these simple people it meant that Twelfth Night fell on what was, by then, January 17th/18th. Wassailing still takes place on and around these dates and is probably a relic and reminder of our old calendar. This is possibly why "white Christmasses" were more common in the past than now, for invariably snowfalls and fierce frosts arrive in early January and not December. The seasons have their own way of working things out.

In large households elaborate parties took place on Twelfth Night which ran on into the following day. Often they eclipsed the actual celebration of Christmas itself, probably because, being a purely secular festival, people felt they could really abandon themselves to pleasurable pursuits not to mention a great deal of eating and drinking. On this night the Yule log was finally extinguished and a charred remnant was carefully stored away to light the log of the following Yuletide. Greenery was stripped off walls, etc. and burnt. It should never be casually discarded on a rubbish heap or in a dustbin, for the gods of fertility will be very cross indeed! No! all greenery must be destroyed and returned to the gods by means of the sacred element of fire or ill-luck could follow.

The only green decoration not thus destroyed was the mistletoe and often the dried up and shrivelled branches were placed up in the rafters of a house to bring good luck and protection from harm by the ancient gods of nature; likewise it was hung in stables and cow byres. A piece of mistletoe placed on a cradle was said to protect a baby from evil spells and harm. Sometimes pieces of dried mistletoe were kept inside a small pouch and worn against a person's body to protect them against sickness and witchcraft. Mistletoe was something of a magical healing plant in the past and it is still used in herbal medicine today.

The Romans believed this plant to be a symbol of peace and fellowship. A truce could be effected by holding out a branch of mistletoe to an enemy. The two opposing leaves on a mistletoe branch are joined together thus making a potent symbol of unity. It is easy to see how stories of this plant's mysterious properties remained with our ancestors and their reasons for preserving those somewhat fossilized remnants as a talisman to "protect" them during the coming year.

Every other single leaf or piece of greenery had to be removed, for it was believed that for every leaf which remained unburnt a goblin would emerge to plague the household.

Robert Herrick writes of this superstition in 1648:

> *Down with the rosemary and so,*
> *Down with the baies and mistletoe,*
> *Down with the holly, ivie, all,*
> *Wherewith ye drest the Christmas hall.*
> *That so the superstitious find*
> *Not one least branch there left behind*
> *For look, how many leaves there be,*
> *Neglected there, maids trust to me*
> *So many goblins you shall see.*

Herrick also supported the medieval belief that the Feast of Christmas should last until Candlemas (February 2nd), i.e. the end of Epiphany. It was, however, the religious festival which was extended rather than the secular one. An old medieval carol says *"Syng we Yole tyl Candlemas"* and as late as 1725 it was recorded that *"the generality of the vulgar continue feasting until Candlemas."* (Bournes Antiquities Vulgares).

The courts held elaborate entertainments on Twelfth Night and very often special plays and masques were written for these costly entertainments. Shakespeare's "Twelfth Night" was first performed at one of these courtly occasions, although the plot has nothing whatever to do with the festival, hence its alternative title of "What You Will".

Samuel Pepys attended a production of this play on January 6th 1663, and records the following comments in his famous diary:

"To the Duke's house, and there saw 'Twelfth Night' acted well, though it be but a silly play and not relating at all to the name or day."

"A Comedy of Errors" was first performed at Grays Inn, London, during the Christmas revels in 1594 under the jurisdiction of the appointed Lord of Misrule. The play has a pantomime-like farcical theme in which mistaken identities and confusion between two separate sets of identical twins causes mayhem amongst the rest of the characters. Being based on an ancient Roman play, The Menaechmi of Plautus, it is not improbable that this piece was performed during the Saturnalian festivities during ancient times. Interestingly, the plot of "Twelfth Night" also turns on twins and the confusion of identities. Role reversal comes into this play when Viola assumes manly garb in emulation of her twin, Sebastian. Elements of pantomime can be traced in these plays which were intended as light-hearted entertainments, although they were stylishly written and contained profound sentiments, which are, of course, lacking in pantos.

Dancing, music, feasting and gambling played a part in these courtly pleasures. Queen Elizabeth loved such revels and in 1597 a somewhat critical report states that:

"At the Twelfe Night revels the head of the Church of England was to be seen in her old age dancing three or four galliards."

At the age of sixty-four Elizabeth's love of dancing seems to have been as great as in her youth.

The courts of James I and Charles I also saw elaborate Twelfth Night productions. Queen Henrietta Maria was an enthusiastic amateur actress appearing in many masques with her ladies. Inigo Jones designed settings and costumes for many of these masques although he was primarily an architect.

When Charles II returned to the throne of Great Britain in 1660 the Christmas celebrations at court were revived. The "Merry Monarch" liked good living, beautiful women and convivial company; he also enjoyed gambling, as John Evelyn notes in his diary:

"According to custom, His Majesty Charles II opened the revels of the night (Twelfth Night) by throwing the dice himself in the Privy chamber, where there was a table set on purpose, and lost his £100. The year before he won £150. The ladies also played very deep. I came away when the Duke of Ormonde had won about £1,000."

Samuel Pepys describes in his diary the customs connected with the Twelfth Night cake which was cut during the party held on that evening: January 6th 1666.

> *"After cards to choose king and queen, and a good cake there was, but no marks found; but I privately found the clove, the mark of the Knave, and privately put it into Captain Cook's piece, which made some mirth, because of his lately being known by his buying clove and mace of the East India prizes. At night, home to my lodging. It being Twelfth Night, they had got the fiddler, and mighty merry they were; and I above, came not to them, leaving them dancing and choosing King and Queen."*

Judging by this extract it would seem that objects, other than a bean and pea which were used to select the king and queen, were also included in the cake to symbolise various additional characters. This was probably the origin of the small silver charms which were used at a later date to denote good luck etc: in our puddings and cakes.

Twelfth Night celebrations continued unabated during the eighteenth century, and in the nineteenth century Leigh Hunt (1784-1859) wrote the following words:

> *"Christmas goes out in fine style - with Twelfth Night. It is a finish worthy of the time.*
>
> *Christmas Day was morning of the season; New Year's Day the middle of it or noon; Twelfth Night is the night brilliant with innumerable planets of Twelfth-cakes. The whole island keeps court, nay all Christendom. All the world are kings and queens. Everybody is somebody else; and at once to laugh at, and to tolerate, characters different from his own by enacting them. Cakes, characters, forfeits, lights, theatres, merry rooms, little holiday faces, and, last but not least, the painted sugar on the cakes, so bad to eat but so fine to look at, useful because it is*

perfectly useless except for a sight and a morsel - all conspires to throw a giddy splendour over the last night of the season...."

As has already been mentioned in a previous chapter, the crowds turned out in great numbers to view these elaborate confections which were displayed in the bakers' windows for the occasion; sometimes they were known as Epiphany Cakes.

It is sad that these Twelfth Night traditions have so completely disappeared and rather puzzling too, considering how recently they continued to be enjoyed. Usually people sieze on any excuse for a good rousing party; how is it that the occasion became dropped from our festive calendar? Our ancestors would have been most surprised by this development.

The Feast of the Epiphany follows Twelfth Night on January 6th, though, as we have already seen, Christmas and Epiphany were once joined together to form the Christmas season ending on February 2nd (Candlemas).

The word Epiphany comes from the Greek EPIPHANEA, which means the manifestation or showing of the Christ Child to the Magi; these Wise Men symbolised the gentiles or the non-Jewish world, thus giving the clear and unmistakable message that Christ came to earth to save all mankind.

The traditional names for the Magi were Melchior, Caspar and Balthasar; they represented the old, the middle-aged and the youthful. One was a white European, another Eastern and the third was black. Some people believe their names to have been Galgath, Magalath and Tharath, and the countries from which they travelled, guided by the Star of Bethlehem, were Nubia, Arabia and Egypt. Others believe that the European king came from Cologne in Germany, and his supposed relics are kept in this splendid Gothic cathedral, having been presented to the city in 1164 by the Emperor Barbarossa (Red-beard). The gifts of gold, frankincense and myrrh symbolized kingship, the god-head or priesthood, and finally suffering and death.

In many countries children believe it is the three kings, or Magi, who bring them their gifts on January 5th/6th, and this is a logical conclusion for young minds to arrive at. Who better than those splendid figures who brought gifts to the infant Christ, to secretly leave gifts for them?

Spanish children put out shoes filled with hay and carrots for the Three King's camels, hoping that the empty shoes will be filled with gifts next morning by Balthasar, the Black King. Probably this has connections with the Moorish occupation of Spain. They also blacken their faces at Epiphany Eve (January 5th) and inspect themselves next morning in the mirror to see if a white patch of skin is showing through where Balthasar kissed them in the night.

In Italy, it is Befana, holding a bell in one hand and a cane in the other, who leaves gifts on Epiphany Eve. She is supposed to have been a woman on whom the Magi called for rest and refreshment. They told her about the Child whom they were journeying to find and invited her to join them in their quest. Like most women she was too busy with household tasks at the time, but promised to follow on after her work was done. Eventually she set out, but never again found the Magi; she was doomed to wander forever searching for the Christ Child and leaving her gifts for children near to the cribs in their homes. People in Czarist Russia believed in a similar figure called BABOUSCHKA (grandmother) about whom a similar story is told. She wanders through the snows searching for Christ and leaving presents for children en route to Bethlehem.

One of the few remaining traditions connected with the Epiphany is held in the Chapel Royal, St.James' Palace, London. In days gone by the reigning sovereign would process in state to the Chapel on January 6th and present gold, frankincense and myrrh to the officiating priest who, in turn, blessed them and offered them up at the altar during the Holy Communion service. Nowadays the monarch is usually represented by one or more of her chamberlains although Prince Charles has attended this ceremony in recent years. The service is frequently presided over by the Bishop of London, Dean of Her Majesty's Chapels Royal. This ancient ceremony symbolised the subjection and homage of an earthly king or queen to the King of Kings. The modern way of doing things makes it all rather second-hand; it is a pity that the reigning monarch no longer attends in person. The public can attend this service and in recent years it has been televised.

Christmas has now well and truly ended with the passing of Twelfth Night, Epiphany and finally Candlemas. The greenery is down, the lights are out, all that remains of the Yule log is a charred stump, kept to awaken the spirit of Yule next year.

Ceremonies for Candlemasse Day

Kindle the Christmas Brand and then
Till Sunne-set, let it burne;
Which, quencht, then lay it up agen
Till Christmas next returne.

Part must be kept wherewith to tend
The Christmas log next yeere;
And where 'tis safely kept, the Fiend,
Can do no mischiefe (there).

Robert Herrick. 1648.

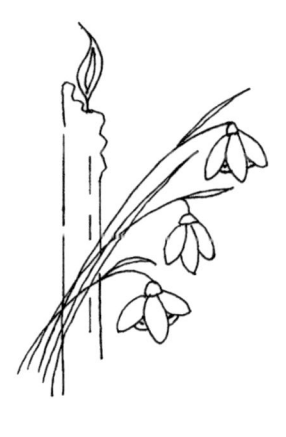

23

NOW BACK to WORK !

PLOUGH MONDAY AND DISTAFF DAY

*God speed the plough,
the plough and the ploughman,
the farm and the farmer,
machine and beast and man.*

An old Plough Monday prayer.

The close of the Christmas festivities on Twelfth Night were followed by rustic ceremonies on Plough Monday (the Monday immediately following Twelfth Night); this ceremony marked the return to work on the land by farmers and labourers. On the previous evening (Sunday) a plough decorated with red ribbons and greenery was carried into the local parish church and left there all night beside the Plough Light in a sort of inanimate vigil. On the Monday morning the local farm-labourers dressed themselves in their best smocks, or shirts, breeches and hats, which had been specially decorated with ribbons and rosettes. One of their number was crudely dressed as a woman, being known as the "Betsy" or "Betty" (it is strange how the male sex have enjoyed dressing up in female guise through the centuries!). Thus arrayed they went to the church and collected the decorated plough after it had been blessed by the priest. In some regions of England, the men who pulled the plough, and hard work it must have been, were known as "Plough Stots" (an old English name for bullock); "Plough Jags" was another title used in the old days.

A decorated plough with a Christmas faggot
(Note the toast for feeding robin)

The plough was then paraded around the village concerned, amidst much hilarity and song. Alms were asked for and anyone refusing to contribute was in danger of having their garden, paths and verges ploughed up by the men. It was a sort of agricultural blackmail, but all in a good cause, for the money collected went towards keeping a candle, or Plough Light, which was kept burning in the church throughout the rest of the year. It was considered a very bad omen for this light to go out, foretelling a disastrous harvest and pestilence amongst the livestock. However, a proportion of these funds was kept as "beer money" for the men on this last fling before the serious business of work began on the following morning. The dish known as frumenty or furmity was very much enjoyed at this time and a large bowl of it was often taken around the village by the Plough Boys. It was made from fresh wheat grains from which the husks had been removed and then boiled in milk with spices until it was of a fairly thick consistency. Sometimes alcohol such as brandy was added and it must have resembled a rather potent porridge similar to the Scottish Athol Brose.

In many areas a corn dolly, made from the last sheaf of wheat gathered in the previous harvest, was ceremoniously ploughed into the soil by the especially decorated plough thus ensuring a continuity of abundance, for the spirit of the last year's crop was transferred into the new spring growth thus forming a chain of fertility down the years.

Interestingly this ceremony can be traced back to the Egyptians, who held similar ceremonies in the sixteen provinces of ancient Egypt. A plough made of tamarisk wood with a share of black copper was used by the priests to plough into the land an image of Osiris which had a face painted green and gold (echoes of our Green Man), and was stuffed with ears of corn. Osiris was the personification of the corn and "died" each year with the harvest and "rose up" again in the spring, bringing new life and plenty. The arabs have a similar custom and bury the "Old Man"; this is actually the last sheaf of wheat to be gathered which returns as the "Young Man" in the new wheat.

Likewise the Scandinavian people made a Yule Boar Loaf from flour of the last sheaf gathered. This carefully modelled loaf was kept right through the Yule Festival and afterwards it was taken out and ploughed into the land.

The Greeks worshipped Dionysus, "he of the green fruit", who was patron of the corn and all fruit bearing trees; he was also believed to have invented the plough, thus saving mankind much drudgery and easing their labours on the land. Legend has it that he was born on a winnowing fan which became one of his symbols. Ceremonies similar to the ones already mentioned occurred during festivals dedicated to him. It can be seen how these pagan rites, concerned with the renewal of growth in the land, have come down to us through thousands of years after being adapted to the needs of succeeding generations. Names and places may change but the symbolism remains unchanged, be the deity Osiris, Dionysus, or even Christ.

Sword dancing by the Morris Men took place during these Plough Monday celebrations which often concluded with the interlocked swords being held over a man's or a "fool's" head, and then they were sharply pulled away in imitation of a beheading which was probably a real, or simulated sacrifice in ages past. Certain mummer's plays were also enacted which contain the character of an old man who is killed by his sons, and then brought back to life again. Whether this symbolises the death of the old year and the coming of the new one, or winter being superseded by fruitful spring, or maybe the death of Christmas which will return again the following year, we do not know.

The Sons:
>Good people all, you see what we have done,
>We have cut our father down like the evening sun
>And here he's all in his purple gore,
>And we are afraid he will never dance more.

Old Man:
>No, no, my children; by chance you are mista'en,
>For here I find myself, I am not slain:
>But I will rise, your sport for to advance,
>And with you all, brave boys, I'll have a dance.

>>Traditional: Revesby Play, Lincolnshire

Women returned to their work on Distaff Day, (January 7th) or the day following Plough Monday, although it is probable that those in domestic service had been hard at work throughout the Twelve Days of Christmas catering for the needs and enjoyment of their employers. No doubt they enjoyed the foolery and fun of Plough Monday as it passed by.

Robert Herrick, (1591–1674) who recorded so many of our rural festivals in the verses contained in his poem Hesperides (1648), wrote the following lines in honour of Saint Distaff's Day:

> Partly worke and partly play,
> Ye must on Saint Distaffe day:
> From the Plough soone free your teame;
> Then come home and fother them.
> If the maids a spinning goe,
> Burne the flax and fire the tow:
>
> Scorch their plackets, but beware
> That ye singe not no maiden-haire.
> Bring in pailes of water then,
> Let the maids bewash the men.
>
> Give Saint Distaffe all the right,
> Then bid Christmas sport good-night.
> And next morrow every one,
> To his own vocation.

(In this instance the women appear to have returned to work on the day after St Distaffe's Day.)

The days of revelry were now well and truly over - unless of course you believed that Christmas ended with Candlemas (February 2nd) as did our medieval forefathers, which must have left everyone with empty pockets and a feeling of utter exhaustion.

It has been said that Charles Dickens invented our modern style Christmas, but this is a fallacy, for it may be seen from the preceding chapters in this book that the traditions which he publicised and promoted existed long before he was born. Being a lover of the festive season he stored up his knowledge of our Yuletide customs and enthusiastically brought them to his readers' notice. Country people especially had never abandoned them. Christmas, as we know it, has slowly evolved over thousands of years, being translated and developed by past generations of many varying beliefs and nationalities. No doubt it will go on evolving and changing in the years to come. It is good to know that Christmas is still alive, well and in good heart.

May future generations continue to enjoy this joyous winter festival with as much pleasure and verve as our ancestors.

> *"Christmas hath made an end, welladay, welladay!*
> *Which was my dearest friend, more is the pity*
> *For with a heavy heart, must I from thee depart*
> *To follow plough and cart, all the year after"*

Traditional

Bibliography

Oxford book of Carols	Percy Dearer, R. Vaughan Williams & Martin Shaw	O.U.P. 1964
The Golden Bough	Sir James George Fraser	MacMillan 1957
A Warwickshire Christmas	David Green	Alan Sutton 1990
The Twelve Days of Christmas	M & J Hadfield	Cassel 1961
In Search of Lost Gods	Ralph Whitlock	Phaidon-Oxford 1979
Customs & Ceremonies of Britain	Charles Kightly	Thames & Hudson 1986
Anatomie of Abuses	Philip Stubbes	1583
Christmas Masque	Ben Jonson	1616
Fantasticks	Nicholas Breton	1626
Histriomastix	William Prynne	1632

The Poems of Robert Herrick (1591 – 1674)

William Bradford's Journal (1620)

Shepherd's Calendar	John Clare	1827
The Illustrated London News		1848

Old Christmas – Sketch Book	Washington Irving	1875
Christmas in Ritual & Tradition	Clement C Miles	1912
Diary of Samuel Pepys	George Bell & Sons	1926
Diaries of John Evelyn (1604-1706)	Ed: by de Beer	Clarendon Press
A Christmas Carol	Charles Dickens	Chapman & Hall 1843
The Renaissance in Italy	John Addington Seymonds 1840-1893	
Christmas at the Manor (Lord Chief Justice Bramston's Gifts)	The Times	December 23rd 1935
Good things in England	Florence White	Jonathon Cape 1932
British Folk Customs	Christine Hale	BCA 1976
Ministry of Food wartime recipe leaflets – 1942/45		
The Night Before Christmas	Clement C Moore	George Harrap 1931

Acknowledgements

'Torches, torches' tr J B Trend (1887-1958) from 'The Oxford Book of Carols' © Oxford University Press 1928. Reproduced by permission. All rights reserved.

'Voisin, d'ou venait' pr Eleanor Farjeon from 'The Oxford Book of Carols' © Oxford University Press 1928. Reproduced by permission. All rights reserved.

The first Christmas card by J. C. Horsley dated 1843, is reproduced by kind permission of © V&A Images and Albert Museum, London.

The Illustration of Queen Victoria's Christmas Tree with accompanying description dated December 1848, is reproduced by kind permission of The Illustrated London News.

The Welsh quotations used in the Mari Lwyd ceremonies from the book "Customs & Ceremonies of Britain" (pages 157) by Charles Kightly, Pub: Thames & Hudson 1986, is reproduced by kind permission of the author.

The Lucy family Christmas at Charlecote Park, part of an article by Sally Rowat (1975), is printed by kind permission of Worcestershire Life, (formally Warwickshire & Worcestershire Life).

The poem "A Countrywoman's Tribute" by Evelyn Knibbs, is reproduced by kind permission of her husband Harold Knibbs, of Marton, Warwickshire.

My thanks to the Somerset Rural Life Museum and the Welsh Folk Museum for their help and assistance.

The author has made every effort to trace copyright owners.